WALKS IN THE
SLOW LANES OF
SUFFOLK

For Cell

Hope you enjoy the walks
that I loved too.

Angie

Published by Sigma Leisure – an imprint of
Sigma Press, Stobart House, Pontyclerc, Penybanc Road, Ammanford, Carmarthenshire SA18 3HP.

British Library Cataloguing in Publication Data
A CIP record for this book is available from the British Library.

ISBN: 978-1-910758-41-0

Typesetting and Design by: Sigma Press, Ammanford.

Cover: Charsfield © Angie Jones

Photographs: © Angie Jones

Maps: © Angie Jones

Printed by: Akcent Media

Disclaimer: the information in this book is given in good faith and is believed to be correct at the time of publication. No responsibility is accepted by either the author or publisher for errors or omissions, or for any loss or injury however caused. Only you can judge your own fitness, competence and experience. Do not rely solely on sketch maps for navigation: we strongly recommend the use of appropriate Ordnance Survey (or equivalent) maps.

WALKS IN THE SLOW LANES OF SUFFOLK

Angie Jones

In memory of my father, Owen Martin who instilled in me a love for the countryside and also of my sister, Julie who shared that love. Both died in 2016.

Also with thanks to God for my dear husband, Maurice (Mogsy), who has tramped these many miles with me.

Acknowledgements

Thank you to the many Suffolk folk who I've met on my journeys, whose stories have enriched my memories of their hamlets and villages and of course to my dear husband for sharing this adventure.

CONTENTS

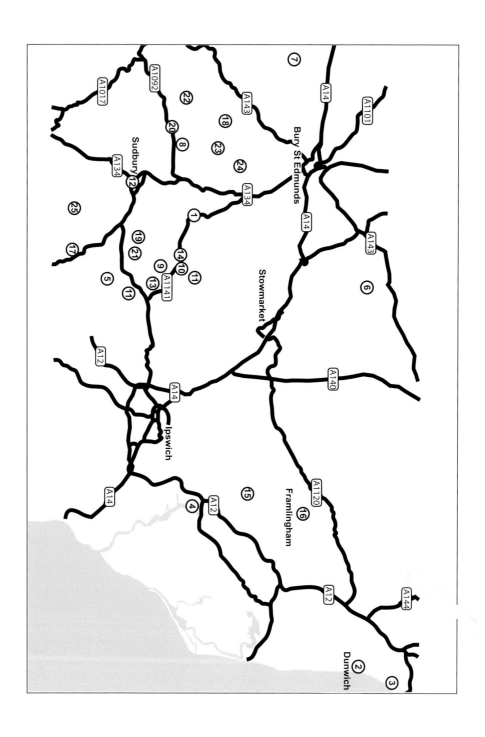

INTRODUCTION

I'm not sure what came first; the love of the Suffolk countryside, walking or writing. But somehow these three things came together to create this, my first book.

Suffolk in essence is farming – a patchwork of fields rising and falling with the gently undulating land. My walks explore tiny hamlets where humble cottages cluster around a country church built from hand-gathered flints or villages full of grand timber-framed houses – evidence of the prosperous woollen cloth trade; or walks that simply explore woodlands, fields and footpaths around isolated farmsteads.

Most of these twenty-five (often circular walks) are less than five miles – many much shorter. They are for people like myself, released from the routine of work, who have time to amble along at a leisurely pace, time to pause and reflect, to simply enjoy the created world around us. So this book seeks to inspire and motivate its readers to wander off the beaten track, to linger in, and learn about these lovely places.

I've included descriptions scribbled down as I walked that way, to give you a taste of what to expect. Often I've stumbled across wonderful characters who, with a smile, have shared their stories and previously unwritten local (often amusing) secrets of the past.

There is a touch of history with snippets of information I've gleaned about the places featured in these walks, and reference to the flowers and trees you might see along the way.

And for a little fun; if you look closely at the photographs you may find the figure of my husband, Maurice – who walked with me, come rain or shine.

And just when your legs are aching – there's mention of a tea-room of pub near and handy for that well deserved rest!

I hope you enjoy exploring Suffolk as much as we did.

Angie Jones

WALK 1: LAVENHAM

Cordwainers

This is a short circular walk that edges around the picture postcard village of medieval Lavenham then takes you into the heart of the town. There are three hundred and twenty buildings of historical interest here for it was once the fourteenth wealthiest town in England – paying more tax than York! Allow time to explore the many art galleries and shops or even to visit the museum.

It isn't just the past that makes Lavenham special. Yes, the streets are full of weird and wonderful Tudor houses, halls and quaint little shops but it's the present too – as I discovered one day.

Distance	1.2 miles or 1.9km
Time	1 hour but allow time for browsing
Start	The car park for the Village Hall just behind The Cock Public House
Terrain	Gentle slopes, mainly level
Map	OS Landranger 155
Refreshments	Spoilt for choice of little cafés, pubs and takeaways
Toilets	In the car park near The Cock Public House
Getting there	By car take the B1115 from Sudbury or find the A1141 which goes through this village. There is a train service to Sudbury and taxis are available. The 753 bus runs from Bury St Edmunds to Sudbury via Lavenham

1. Start at the end of the main street near the church. Here you can leave your car. The sign in the car park behind 'The Cock' says: 'No tickets. No Clamps. No fines.' Instead we are invited to make a donation in the box. How kind. There are also good maps for visitors here by the public loos, so every need is catered for as you start your exploration of this wonderful, old town.

Lavenham church

Cross the road, heading towards the impressive wool church of St Peter and Paul built in 1525 with its 43 metre high landmark of a tower and follow the footpath sign. This takes you to Potland Lane edged with sun-warmed brick walls where moss grows amidst the scramble of brambles.

2. The road curves and soon you will pass Lavenham Hall, a 16th century timbered framed house, standing in its lovely garden with statues of animals half hidden among the shrubs.

3. At Park Road bear left and soon you will see a stile on the right which leads into open countryside.

It was a day in late February when I explored Lavenham. I noticed the hint of spring in the air; noisy birdsong, catkins and lichened-stained branches swelling with buds. Rooks cawed, high in tall trees and pale, but welcome sunshine lit up last year's straggly grass and in the sky a buzzard soared as I tramped across a meadow. In the middle of a muddy patch was the next stile, I was glad I'd got my boots on.

4. Go over the stile and wander across the field towards the hedge line marking the old railway line. Bear right. Untidy woodland with fallen trees and broken branches borders the path but soon you will see the railway bridge ahead. Turn right again cross a small stream and you come back into the village. Turn right. As you make your way back, note the terraced cottages lining the busy road and bearing the name of Roper. You will see Roper's Court on the spot where a horsehair factory employed local girls and women in the 19th century.

5. Across the road in an unassuming red brick house is The Contemporary Gallery . For lovers of Art – this is a must! Paul Evans decided he would be an artist – about the age of eight. A good decision!

The Swan Hotel and street scene

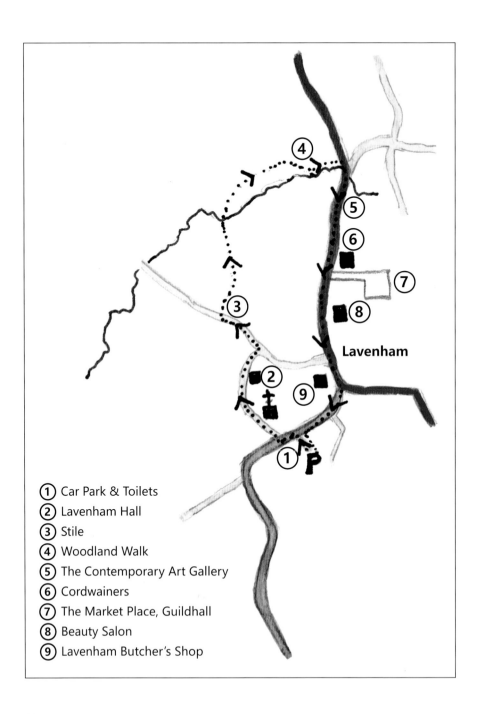

Lavenham

1. Car Park & Toilets
2. Lavenham Hall
3. Stile
4. Woodland Walk
5. The Contemporary Art Gallery
6. Cordwainers
7. The Market Place, Guildhall
8. Beauty Salon
9. Lavenham Butcher's Shop

The Gallery opens most days, but do check before you visit. Paul himself is often there – ready to chat to customers. There is a good range of cards and prints if you aren't rich enough to buy an original. Every November Paul launches a new exhibition so this is a good time to visit.

"My work has always reflected my love for remote rural areas ... I absorb all the sights, sounds and smells while I paint." Colourful tangles of wild flowers, untrodden snowy fields, deep shadowy forests and the sparkle of the sea beyond wide stretches of sand are all framed against the walls. Some of the pictures were painted locally.

6. Further along the street, where the fragrance of food wafts from assorted little cafes, I see Cordwainers – in Suffolk pink, once the One Bell Inn and later a shoe-makers. Like many timbered buildings it was built of green wood. As it dried the walls became warped and this is a fine example of wonky house – sideways on!

7. Market Lane leads to Market place dominated by The Guildhall of Corpus Christi – a fine building dating from 1529 now owned by the National Trust. It was once used as a prison but now houses a museum about local history, including trades and people. There is a walled garden where plants used for dye are still grown. Check opening times as they tend to change.

Opposite is a tiny old-fashioned bakery, Sparling and Faiers. This Suffolk family have been baking bread since the 17th^h century.

When I did this walk I stepped inside and met Ann Faiers. She told me that her grandfather was a baker and her sons are too. "I make the wedding cakes", she said. There are gingerbread men and women, and ginger cats for sale but I settled for a sugary, creamy doughnut – with a faraway taste of childhood.

8. Continue down the main street passing intriguing little shops where you may choose to linger.

When I walked here there was a Wildlife Art Gallery. I stepped inside to see wonderful carvings and pottery, as well as colourful, bold linocuts of animals and birds. Here I was in for a surprise! On a picture where a tractor ploughs and gulls swoop, I noticed the artist's signature – Andrew Haslan. Hmm? There was something familiar about that name. Fifty years ago in my class at school there was boy who loved to draw birds. He had a little sketch book full of goldcrests and herons, bullfinches and wrens. All the children admired his skill. I wondered?

I tentatively approached a man sitting behind a desk. Yes, it was Andrew. How amazing! A self-taught artist, his work ranges from pencil sketches of woodpeckers to bold lino cuts of black-edged hares. I asked him how he mastered lino-cuts so effectively.

"Don't you remember potato prints at school?" he said with a smile, "it all started there".

The Wildlife Gallery has closed recently and is now a Beauty Salon attached to The Swan Hotel, but Andrew's work is still seen in the other art galleries in Lavenham and indeed throughout East Anglia.

9. Walk past the much-photographed Swan Hotel which offers accommodation if you wish to extend you visit. A little further along – on the other side of the road you will see under its black awnings, the award winning Lavenham Butcher's Shop – recently re-opened by new business partners, Gareth and Greg.

The shop was busy selling black treacle bacon and venison sausages but they found time to talk between customers. Both men were Saturday boys for local butchers. Greg trained as a chef but became interested in meat. He is now a licensed deer-stalker as is his wife, Jenny. Everything they sell is from good local sources; free range pork from Blythburgh and free-range chickens from Phil Truin.

"We make all our own sausages", said Greg, proudly. The glazed Lavenham pasties looked delicious. There is local jam and honey on sale too. Before I said goodbye the men posed outside for a photo, wearing their aprons as well as cheeky grins.

A short stroll up the hill will take you back to the car park where you began. Don't forget the donation box – but save some pennies for the picture you'd like to buy one day when you're rich.

WALK 2: DUNWICH

An easy walk exploring Dunwich and its history; following pathways through clifftop woodlands and along country roads. It includes a visit to the informative museum.

A drive through the leafy forest of Dunwich with it Corsican pines, birch and poplar trees brings you to the main street of this now tiny settlement of about one hundred souls.

But had you travelled through time you would have seen a vastly different place, indeed in the 13th century it was the sixth most important town in England and all because of the sea, which is ironic because it was the sea and the shifting shingle that caused the demise of this once prosperous harbour with its ship-building yard and forty-plus fishing boats. A brisk trade with the continent flowed from Dunwich – exporting wool, corn and salted fish and bringing back wine, long before anyone thought of the EU.

In one night in 1286 a great storm choked the deep navigational channels and within a few years Dunwich had dwindled. The Black Death in 1348 furthered the decline. Attempts to clear the shingle failed and in 1589 the villagers gave up their battle. The sea had won!

Coastal erosion carried houses and churches away with the tides – the last church; 'All Saints' finally toppling over the crumbling cliff in 1919. So for history lovers, Dunwich is a must for visitors to Suffolk.

Distance	1.5 miles or 2.4 km
Time	Approximately 1 hour
Start	Free car park by the Fish and Chip Café
Terrain	Path through woodland is quite steep, but mainly even
Map	OS Explorer 231
Refreshments	Fish and Chip Café by the sea The Ship in the main street (also offers overnight accommodation)
Toilets	By the car park
Getting there	By car: from A12 several small roads lead to Dunwich – 11 miles north of Aldeburgh and 9 miles south of Southwold

1. If you drive down St James Street you eventually arrive at the sea and a free car park. Here is the famous black weather-boarded café, with plenty of picnic tables for an authentic fish and chip dish, breathing in sea air and the fragrance of vinegar while gazing across the wide open salt marshes. A sign says, "Do Not Feed the Seagulls!"

Waiters and waitresses in green polo shirts are busy carrying plates laden with food or clearing away empty plates.

Back on the road bear left to find a footpath sign (Sanderlings Walk) that takes you up a steep path through trees. On the right are the stone walls of the Franciscan Priory built in 1290. On the left is the sea. You can hear the roar of the waves crashing below but are warned not to go too near to the cliff edge.

In light of the history of this place I think that is wise!

2. You will come to a gap, which gives access to the Grey Friars Priory walls. What a huge site this is! There are arched doorways and windows of the refectory and the 14th century gateway and the remaining stone walls surround a stretch of grass.

3. Further along the path, look for a tombstone on your left – the only surviving grave of All Saints cemetery. Jacob Forster, who died on 12th March 1796 aged 38, is hanging on for dear death not far from the cliff edge. I wonder how long before he too will be lost to the sea?

   Beyond a gateway a yellow arrow points right. Go through the wooden gate and follow a path with thick nettles beneath trees to your left and the boundary wall on your right. Then turn left into the woodland where

Salt marches

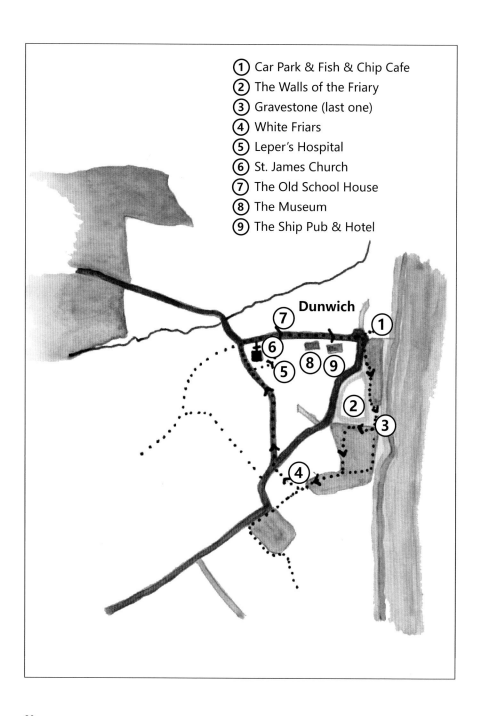

1. Car Park & Fish & Chip Cafe
2. The Walls of the Friary
3. Gravestone (last one)
4. White Friars
5. Leper's Hospital
6. St. James Church
7. The Old School House
8. The Museum
9. The Ship Pub & Hotel

Dunwich

brown leaf litter softens your footsteps and tall Holm oaks and sweet chestnuts block out the sun.

At another gate, where a board announced Grey Friars Wood, bear left along a well-trodden path towards houses. A white-painted iron gate bearing a friar motif appears on your left.

4. At 'White Friars' a yellow arrow directs walkers right along a path that squeezes between overgrown elm hedges.

When I did this walk I soon realised that nettles and brambles were out to get me. I took great care to avoid their caress and was relieved to reach the road, an un-stung hero!

Turn right at the road, then immediately left, where a sign points to St James Church. Yes, further along this lane there is a remaining church – built inland on safer ground!

This is a quiet road – with little traffic, which is good as there are no pavements. Spindly trees overhang from high banks on either side as the road drops down to Church Farm, with its collection of barns with sagging roofs and mossy steps leading to a hayloft.

5. Then you come to St James church itself, standing amidst tall lime trees.
& It was built in 1830 and restored in 2009. The last buttress from the lost
6. All Saints Church stands in one corner of the churchyard – to remind us of the past. Take time to enjoy the peace of this country church.

I was drawn to the some ancient ruins which in 1206 served as a hospital for people with leprosy which was quite common in England at that time. Some twenty men and women were cared for here – away from the community. The last leper was buried in 1536. After that the hospital was used for aged and infirm until it fell into disrepair and was abandoned in 1685. If only the stones in these walls could speak; they could tell a story or two. Instead I make do with the information boards.

A party of students were hovering around the church porch, having, 'their minds blown away' by a confident, enthusiastic teacher. I left them to it and wandered through the churchyard with old leaning gravestones in a sea of red poppies.

The remains of the Leprosy Hospital

7. Turn right onto the road where the faraway landscape of salt marshes stretches out before you; simply miles of emptiness and space.

   Soon you will see cottages edging the road; The Old School; The Old Forge; Jasmine Cottage and Rose Cottage with (in summer) baskets of flowers hanging from a fruit tree in the garden.

8. Then you will see the museum across the road where the generous benefactor, Colonel Michael Barnes, stares down upon visitors from his framed portrait. It is housed in a cottage in the main street and a board outside welcomes visitors. Admission is free but donations are invited and I soon discovered that it's well worth an hour or two if you have time to spare. There is a model of

The Museum

Dunwich, showing it before and after the storm and pictures explaining the shifting coastline as well as chronologically sequenced display cases with treasures found in the sands and cliffs over the years. A photo shows divers proudly showing treasures found beneath the surging waves.

The Ship Hotel

When I was there a lady behind the desk readily answered questions and told me that yesterday there had been one hundred and five visitors and that today was already up to eighty one. I was interested to learn about Robert Woolner, who had lived at a farm in Dunwich until 1836 when he and his wife, three children, two horses and cattle, together with farm implements emigrated to the New World. The weather was bad which meant they were at sea for seventy-two days – with supplies running low they kept themselves and their animals alive with ship's biscuits and beer! One daughter, Lucy Ann became the grandmother of Lucy Maud Montgomery – author of the children's book; 'Anne of Green Gables'. She came to Dunwich for her honeymoon and stayed at The Ship Inn.

9. Outside turn right and head back to the car. You will pass The Ship (once the Barne Arms), a substantial red-bricked pub/hotel offering overnight accommodation as well as a restaurant for day-trippers.

My short walk ends here, but don't forget to allow time to stroll along the shore and even take off your shoes for a paddle in the cold sea, which after all has shaped Dunwich over the tides of time.

WALK 3: WALBERSWICK

Today a small settlement perched on the mouth of the Blyth, Walberswick was a major trading port until the First World War. It is situated in an Area of Outstanding Natural Beauty of heathland and marshes. This is a gentle stroll along the coast, by the estuary and through the village itself.

Stop briefly to view the church of St Andrews – the fourth one for this village built in the ruins of a much bigger one from the days when Walberswick knew prosperity. (In the churchyard the signs warn visitors to keep a safe distance from the broken walls in case of falling masonry.)

In the 13th century, boats sailed from this estuary carrying fish, cheese, corn and timber. By the 14th century there was a fleet of ships trading with Europe,

St Andrew's Church

Iceland and outlying islands. But with a changing coastline and shifting silt, channels became shallow and navigation difficult. Trade lessened and the town declined.

Back in the car drive down The Street (once called Fish Street), to this lovely seaside village with its fishing boats, cottages and tea shops, clustering together where the river meets the sea.

Distance	1.5 miles or 2.4 km
Time	Approximately 1 hour
Start	Car park by sand dunes. £3 all day
Terrain	Level, but some walking on shingle beach
Map	OS Explorer 231
Refreshments	A choice of tea shops and pubs including The Black Dog (Deli), The Parish Lantern, The Bell and The Anchor
Toilets	Public toilets by the village hall
Getting there	A short drive from the A12 along the B1387 brings you to Walberswick, one mile from its neighbour Southwold and eleven miles South of Lowestoft. There is a bus service from Saxmundham but you have to book a seat. The nearest railway station is in Haleworth. Take the B1387 and you'll soon find yourself driving past the free range pork snoozing in the sun or rooting in the mud. Then you'll come to bracken edged woodland before you see the church tower heralding Walberswick – the home and harbour of Saxon Waldbert

1. By the village hall and public toilets, a narrow track crossing the flood gates leads to a car park. It costs £3 for the whole day. Head for the sea!

I walked across the deep softness of the sand dunes, (with boarded-up black beach huts, with their rusty padlocks), drawn by the roar of crashing waves

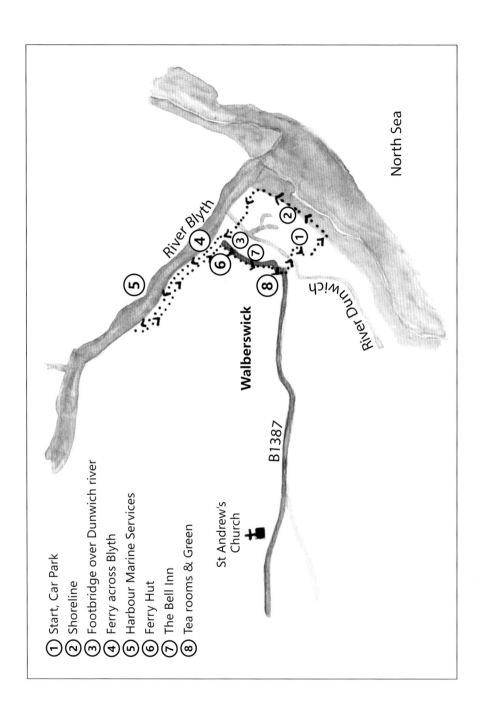

① Start, Car Park
② Shoreline
③ Footbridge over Dunwich river
④ Ferry across Blyth
⑤ Harbour Marine Services
⑥ Ferry Hut
⑦ The Bell Inn
⑧ Tea rooms & Green

St Andrew's Church

Walberswick

B1387

River Blyth

River Dunwich

North Sea

to the sea. I crunched over the shingle that moved and rolled beneath my boots. People sheltered behind bright blue, plastic windbreaks while I marched into the wind and felt the whipped-up salt spray on my face from the metallic-silver water.

2. Turn left and follow the shore line with Southwold before you, sitting on the horizon beyond the salt marshes and reed beds. You come to the River Blyth which blocks your path. Head inland, back across the dunes into quietness as the sea is left behind.

A rough concrete road leads to a wooden bridge where they're all at it! Crabbing!

I watched grandpas, mums and excited, sun-hatted children. "Dad, I've got one!" came a yell. As I stared, an escapee scuttled sideways across the planks and dropped back to safety with a gentle splash. Others, trapped in translucent tubs of murky water circled endlessly, searching for way out. Gulls were hovering and swooping in, looking for an easy meal.

Until recently Walberswick hosted an annual Crabbing Competition every August. Then it got silly. In 2009 there were 1,252 entrants who flooded

The salt marshes

into the little town to spend ninety minutes trying to catch the heaviest crab. The car parks, roads and rivers simply couldn't cope – not to mention the crabs, so now it's just for fun. (Unless you happen to be a crab, of course!)

3. Cross the smaller river Dunwich and bear right towards the Blyth.

As I approached the harbour the landscape became was busy with people. Families clustered by the water, with all the paraphernalia of a day by the sea; pushchairs, picnic baskets, back-packs and buckets, fishing nets and rods. Squawking gulls wheeled and dived overhead. By black weather-boarded huts an information board told me about the Harbour (the Wyc). In summer brightly painted red fishing boats bring home bass and flat fish and in autumn – sprats, cod and herring.

Fishing boats and huts

4. Follow the river inland along a raised tow path. Look out for the Ferry – which has been rowed faithfully between March to October by five generations of the same family. In 1956 the ferry man was eighty-four year old Bob Cross who was born and bred in Walberswick. Prior to rowing the ferry, Bob had been a fisherman on trawlers from Lowestoft.

Before the First World War a pontoon ferry had carried horses and carts across the Blyth – saving the seven mile road journey to Southwold.

I watched the ferryman push away from the jetty and row upstream to be carried back by the strong current as he took his passengers to the far side. A licence for a ferry was granted in the 13th century. (If you cross here, just for the fun of it, there is a footbridge inland, to bring you back.)

Walk along a high bank. On the left cattle (intent on breakfast) heads down, edge forward tearing up mouthfuls of grass. Their tails flick from side to side.

5. On your right are the boats with discordant clanking bells and rolled up sails, trembling rigging and fluttering flags. Yellowy seaweed is draped

from mooring ropes that disappear into the depths. Outboard motors are hoisted askew and ropes like coiled up snakes, adorn the jetties. A big warehouse bearing the words Harbour Marine Services Ltd. comes into view.

On my stroll I decided to retrace my steps but the path does lead inland to Bailey Bridge where you can cross on foot to the far bank – and walk back to the Ferryman to bring you over the river, if you feel like more of an adventure!

Across the river is a line of fisherman's huts, beyond the boats; LT 442; LT 230 and 'Sidney Bates'. A sign sticks up in the water; DEAD SLOW. The wind rustles the reed beds and I notice the marine flowers edging my path; clumps of sea purslane, with tiny greeny-yellow flowers, daisy-like sea mayweed; purple mallow and spikes of sea holly.

6. At the ferry hut, where you can buy a book and see old photos, follow the path right towards the village. When you see a car park to your left, turn right. (A sign points to the toilets.) You will see a terrace of lovely old cottages – full of character.

A terrace of cottages

On a wall outside there were boxes of old books for sale in aid of the Cystic Fibrosis Fund. Some titles reflected Walberswick, where half of the properties are holiday homes; 'The Hidden Oasis'; 'The Take-Over' and 'Whatever you Love'. Plaques on walls indicate Heritage Hideaways or Wally Webb, Builder of Walberswick worked here. 1946-2012.

7. Wander through the houses and you will come to the six hundred year Bell Inn serving Adnams Ale and open for lunch from 12.00 to 2.30. Then pass Todd's cottage made of rounded pebbles where, in July, a red rose entwined itself around the window. Look out for a VR post box in the wall as you approach the village green where children pendulum back and forth on squeaky swings. Assorted houses keep an eye on the comings and goings.

8. Bear left and in summer you will see hollyhocks and pale pink hydrangeas peeking over a low wall by the Old Tea Room. There are several little shops and cafés. The Parish Lantern is crammed full of knick-knacks; keepsakes for a dusty shelf at home to remind you of your day by the sea. Tea and iced drinks are served here, in a pretty patio garden. This is a sheltered place to sit on a sun-warmed bench with a dribbling ice-cream. The Black Dog Deli, around the corner is known for its good coffee and home-made quiches too.

Across the road near a bus shelter is the starting point, the village hall and public loos. A left turn takes you back to the car park along a track.

My stroll had not been strenuous, only 2.4 km or about 1.5 miles. I decided to dump my camera in my car. I took off my boots, to feel the silky sand as I crossed the dunes, then I winced over the stones and at last let my feet cool in the swirling sea.

Walk 4: Woodbridge

Woodbridge is one of my favourite places for an afternoon treat. It is a place to dawdle and linger. Echoes of the past meet you wherever you turn; Tudor, Georgian, Regency and Victorian buildings jostle for space along narrow lanes or look over the Market Square with its Elizabethan Shire Hall which houses two museums.

Then there is The Thoroughfare, voted as a top ten UK high street in 2013 by the 'Sunday Times' with little family-run shops full of the interesting and unusual. But perhaps most important is the estuary of the river Deben with a plethora of boats and an exhilarating by stroll the silvery waterside – a must for bird-watchers!

Distance	A 'there- and-back' walk along the sea-wall by the estuary. 1.5.miles or 2.4km but add another half a mile to explore around the town itself
Time	Just under one hour for the estuary walk
Start	There are several car parks. The one by the station is handy for this walk
Terrain	Level throughout but there is a footbridge across the railway. There are crossing gates a little further along if the steep steps are difficult
Map	OS Explorer 212
Refreshments	Plenty of cosy little cafés, pubs and restaurants as well as takeaways. The Tea Hut by the water's edge offers snacks and wonderful milk shakes. Ye Old Bell and Steelyard – claiming to be the oldest inn in town has local ale and home-cooked food
Toilets	Public loos near the station car park and further along the water's edge
Getting there	Come how you like! Catch a 64 bus from Ipswich or an hourly train from London; come by road from the A12; sail up river to the Tide Mill and moor your boat for 24 hours for free; or come by foot along the Sandlings walk (all 55 miles) – as it threads its way through an area of outstanding natural beauty and along the Suffolk coast into Woodbridge itself

1. From the A12 the B1079 takes you right into Woodbridge, passing delightful houses on the way to the car park by the station. This is a good location for both the walk by the estuary and the town itself. From here an iron footbridge is the quickest route to the water front. Do pause to enjoy the much changed scenery from this bridge.

I am in a different landscape; a picture of wide grey water edged with mud flats; big skies and everywhere – boats. Moored houseboats; chugging motor boats; graceful Bermudan sloops; yawls and ketches; rowing boats, canoes and tiny dinghies and if you're lucky – a Thames sailing barge and beyond them the back drop of the white weather-boarded Tide Mill.

The Mill beyond the moorings

The path follows the curve of the river Deben where hunched-up swans wait hopefully for crusts of bread. If the tide is out there are stretches of grey mud scored with footprints of birds. If you choose to sit and stare across the stretch of water there are plenty of benches along the route. You will see Woodbridge boatyard on your right which provides winter mooring for over one hundred and fifty yachts and motor boats.

2. Soon you come to The Tea Hut (open all year but not on Mondays) and the public toilets.

As I entered the little café the smell of hot sausage rolls greeted me. I succumbed – and enjoyed the delicious taste of sausage meat laced with oregano, onion and tomato puree – in a crisp brown pastry. I indulged too in a tall glass of ice-cream milk shake – opting for honeycomb and caramel. Then I continued my walk by the river where white gulls squawked and bickered over titbits and a boat chugged out to sea, its waves causing mallard ducks to bob up and down as if riding a carousel.

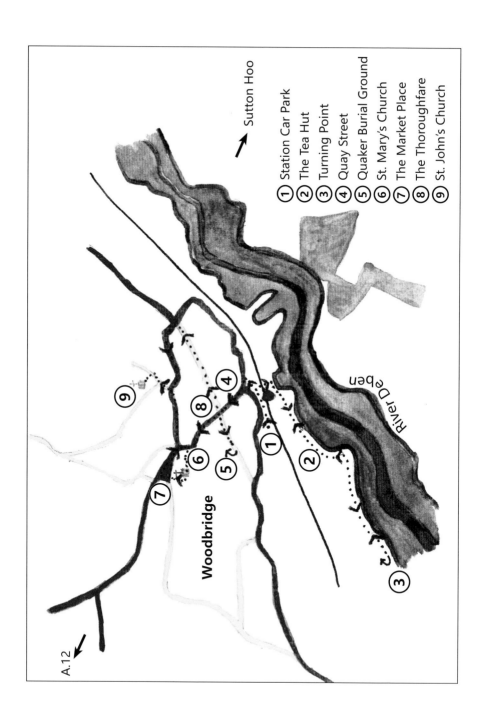

Sutton Hoo

① Station Car Park
② The Tea Hut
③ Turning Point
④ Quay Street
⑤ Quaker Burial Ground
⑥ St. Mary's Church
⑦ The Market Place
⑧ The Thoroughfare
⑨ St. John's Church

River Deben

Woodbridge

A.12

Back on the walk look out for information boards telling you about the rich bird life – apparently over one hundred and fifty different species of birds can be seen here.

A curlew prodded the mud with his long beak and lapwings called as they flew low over the water.

3. You will eventually reach trees and here you could take another footpath straight back into the town or simply retrace your steps, as I did, enjoying another view of the estuary. The view is lovely, so take your time.

Masts stood tall with flags fluttering aloft. Sails are furled – awaiting release in the keen wind. Ropes hung slack attached to bright orange marker buoys and everywhere the sound of little ship's bells clanking and jangling.

The impressive 1793 Tide Mill is open during summer months, and

The Estuary

for a donation you can clamber up the wooden ladder-like stairs and learn about the days when it was a working mill. There are still demonstrations of flour making on some days. You will need to make a detour from my suggested walk but, if time, it is well worth a visit.

4. Cross back over the iron footbridge and make you way over a zebra crossing then up Quay Street as you head into the town. When you come to a crossroads go straight over into Church Street.

5. For a short detour, look out for a narrow road on your left – Turn Lane. Down here is a Quaker burial ground, behind a barred wooden gate. It is a place of stillness and serenity, a place to pause and perhaps pray. The simple grave of Bernard Barton, a bank clerk who was an aspiring poet, stands among the long seeding grasses.

The harbour

6. Back in Church road you come to flint-faced St Mary's Church with its 108 feet high tower. It has been used as a place of worship for over six hundred years. In the porch is the 1635 bread cupboard where loaves were left for the poor people *on the bread line* every Sunday. Inside you will find the tomb of Thomas Seckford – a benefactor and a lawyer at the court of Queen Elizabeth I. Look too for the photograph of George Denman-Dean, killed in 1917.

   Outside amongst the headstones is the grave of John Clarkson – who campaigned against slavery. You will see some steps into an alley way that leads to Market Hill.

7. Market Hill is the centre of the town. It houses Woodbridge Museum, open 10-4 daily. Here chronological displays tell the story of Woodbridge from Anglo Saxon times to present day. Shire Hall – once an Elizabethan Courthouse and corn market is open for guided tours on Sunday afternoons. Look too for the violin shop where violins are both made and sold. The King's Head serves food and Adnam's Ales. Hill House Hall offers bed and breakfast if you'd like a weekend away.

8. You have a choice of roads to explore from here. The Thoroughfare has a bakery, opened in 1946, where creamy cakes and unusual loaves of bread such as Suffolk Crunch may tempt you across the threshold. There is a chocolate shop, a sweetie shop, a kitchen-ware shop as well as cosy little cafés.

9. If you come on a Sunday morning, the local churches invite you to varying styles of worship. At St. Mary's, the huge central church with Thetford flint-work, there is Holy Communion at 8.00 am and parish Eucharist at 10.00; while St John's, the Victorian church on the hill, offers the 9.00 Reflective Time; followed by a mix of traditional and contemporary at 11.00 with a modern style praise and response with various musicians and a digital organ. There's also a Salvation Army, several chapels and a Roman Catholic Church.

If you find nearby Elmhurst Park which has won a Green Flag Award for twelve successive years, this is a lovely place for a picnic on sunny days.

On the way back to the car you'll see the Riverside Theatre, which serves as a cinema, where you can have a 'Meal and Ticket Deal' using the adjoining restaurant if you wish to prolong your visit to Woodbridge – or you can call into the Whistle-Stop railway café and even stay overnight!

Finally I must mention Sutton Hoo – just across the Deben. This is a 255 acre estate with beautiful views of the river. Here you can wander in woodlands, see ancient burial mounds and learn about the Anglo Saxon ship unearthed here in 1939, full of priceless jewellery, drinking horns and silver that was somehow missed by treasure hunters over the centuries. There is an exciting reconstruction of the burial chamber of an Anglo Saxon king. It is open at weekends during winter, but in March will be open every day. Guided tours last for two hours. Entry for National Trust members is free.

Walk 5: Polstead

In the 'Imperial Gazetter' of 1870 there was a population of over nine hundred people living in Polstead in over two hundred houses. Today you will find a much smaller village but still with a lively community and well worth a visit. Every summer local bands play in a music festival. It really consists of five separate little hamlets. In the nineteenth century it became famous for its cherry orchards growing Polstead black cherries.

This is a circular walk that starts and ends in the village going along narrow lanes and across pastures with stiles and kiss gates.

I visited Polstead, a village between Hadleigh and Sudbury, on one of those perfect autumn mornings when the cloudless sky was brilliant blue and the rose-hip berries glowed red in the hedgerow amidst tangles of silvery old man's beard.

Distance	2.2 miles or 3.4 km
Time	Allow an hour or so
Start	Beside the central village green
Terrain	Some ups and downs – in places steep
Map	OS Explorer 196
Refreshments	The Cock Inn and the community shop (for a picnic)
Toilets	A public toilet at the church
Getting there	By car turning from the A1071 near Boxford or from the B1068 at Stoke by Nayland

1. Around the village green is a cluster of houses and cottages as well as the community shop, so here is a good place to leave your car.

   My first stop was the community shop which opens every morning, where two black Labradors were waiting patiently by the door. Inside the shelves were stacked high with groceries – including Lavenham bread; camomile infusion; treacle tart and apple and ginger chutney. The man behind the counter was very happy to chat.

   "Polstead had been without a shop for ten years. There was a local initiative to re-introduce one and it opened in 1984 in a second-hand caravan situated in an old apple orchard. The enterprise attracted national publicity on both the television and radio.

   In 1987 after intense fund-raising, when villagers loaned money to the project, volunteers built an extension to the village hall and here it is today complete with Post Office, still run by a team of willing volunteers and we do well. Daphne's cakes sell like ... hot cakes." says Richard, with a grin. I thanked him and left clutching a cake to give me energy for the walk.

2. But it is time to explore. Walk down the hill passing a thatched cottage where Charles Cheston, a painter lived from 1939 to 1960. He once

exhibited in The Royal Academy. Opposite is 'The Cobblers' another picture postcard cottage. A big timber framed house called Corders is on your left. *I wonder if there's any connection to the infamous William Corder?*

A pretty cottage called The Cobblers

3. You will see a big pond on your right, with benches around it. Follow the curve of its wall around the still water then cross the road where a sign points you to St Mary's Church. Beyond white iron gates crunch up a steep, stony drive and soon you'll be standing in the churchyard.

What a beautiful setting! To the east, beyond one of the biggest war memorials in England, the hedged fields and woodland rise gently to the hills of Nayland, while sheep quietly graze in the nearer pastures.

St Mary's church

4. St Marys, a 12th century Norman church with the only surviving mediaeval stone spire in Suffolk, is delightful. It was carefully restored in 1859. The church gate is grade I listed.

The door was unlocked and I stepped inside where the cool white walls contrasted with ancient red-brick arches. These are not re-used Roman bricks but real very early English bricks, perhaps the oldest to survive in the whole of the country? The brick font sits on a 13th century base. There is an old brass (1460) dedicated to a priest on the north wall. But the secret to the original Norman entrance is in the bell tower! I went through the door and looked back to see a wonderful arch with three bands of heavy chevrons. There is also a public toilet here.

5. Outside, not far from the tower is a simple, wooden shed. Look closer and you will see a plaque;

> *Near this place lay the remains of Maria Marten*
> *who died in the Red Barn, Polstead.*
> *Buried on April 20th 1828 age 25 years. Rest in Peace.*

Maria Marten daughter of the village mole-catcher was murdered by William Corder, son of a local farmer. The lovers had arranged to meet at the Red Barn with the intention of eloping to Ipswich. Maria's family became suspicious when they heard nothing from their daughter. One night her step-mother had a dream – that Maria was buried in the Red Barn. Upon investigation her decomposing body was found in a sack hidden in a grain storage bin, William Corder's green handkerchief around her neck! In 1828 he was hanged in Bury St Edmunds. The story became so well known that souvenir hunters began to chip away at Maria's headstone until it was removed, replaced by this wooden plaque on the shed!

There is another interesting commemorative tablet (1996) here bearing the name of Percy Edwards. He was a respected ornithologist who imitated birdsong and animal calls. He was a story-teller on *Play School* and apparently, the voice of the roaring lion on the Campbells meatballs advertisement! Now there's a claim to fame!

As I leave the churchyard I see another headstone bearing the name of Alexander James Sowman, 32 and his wife Jane, 29. They both died 1907 leaving five children; the youngest, Rosa only 4 months old. Alexander was

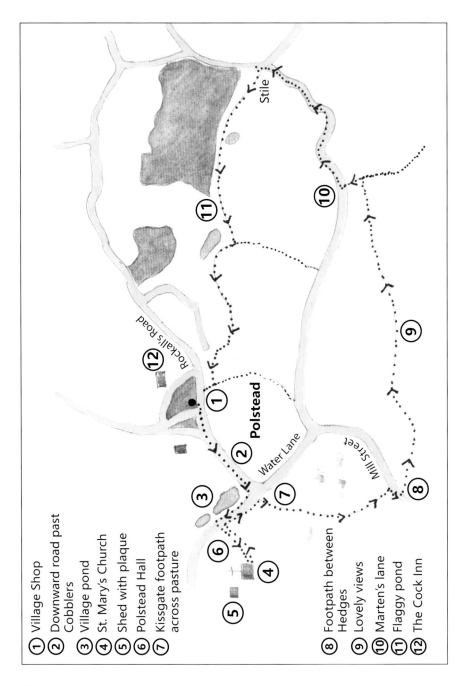

Polstead

Rockall's Road

Water Lane

Mill Street

Stile

1. Village Shop
2. Downward road past Cobblers
3. Village pond
4. St. Mary's Church
5. Shed with plaque
6. Polstead Hall
7. Kissgate footpath across pasture
8. Footpath between Hedges
9. Lovely views
10. Marten's lane
11. Flaggy pond
12. The Cock Inn

born in Polstead and worked on the land but they were married for only nine years. I wonder what terrible tragedy befell this little family?

6. As you double back down the gravel drive towards the road, through the trees on the left you can catch glimpses of Polstead Hall – an impressive Georgian house built in 1819.

7. Turn right down the road and return to the junction where a kiss gate (left) leads to a footpath across the pasture you have just gazed upon. Stop to look back to see the church with its 1980s aluminium roof that shines in the sunlight.

   On the day I was here there was a gentle breeze stirring the warm air as I strode across the meadow where the sheep rested in the shade.

8. As the meadow ends you cross a stream and then a road. Bear right past 'The Plantation' and look for the footpath on the opposite side that squeezes between two thick hedges, just by Polstead Lodge. Follow this path which leads into rough grazing land where black elderberries were heavy in the hedges and the wind chased thistledown across the grass.

9. Follow a trodden path that dips and climbs up to an oak tree where acorns are strewn in the grass. Here a wooden sign directs you right but first pause to enjoy the lovely view. (If you have time take a short detour here to a bench where you can overlook the village in its lovely setting.)

10. At a kiss gate take the path between paddocks, passing a massive, fairly new house with a slate roof, down in the valley to the right until you come to a restricted by-way. Here turn left, then right into leafy Marten's Lane. Pollarded trees line the banks where rabbit holes disappear into blackness.

    Soon you bear left towards Hadleigh. A few steps will bring you to the next footpath sign, hidden in a hole in the hedge on the left. To your right is a paddock and another house.

    There follows several stiles, cackling geese at a pond and a wooden bridge before you find yourself walking beside woodland where a small stream trickles. You may hear a jay screeching. In early autumn watch out for brown hawker dragonflies zinging across your path.

11. Bear right to Flaggy Pond at another kiss gate and walk through a tunnel of blackthorn where purple sloes gleam from overhanging branches. A metal gate leads to a meadow and the village again where solar panels shine on rooftops. Skirt the field edge and then cross the pasture to a far gate. By a house on the edge of a small estate called 'Knovak' you can cut back to the green.

My final stop was 'The Cock Inn', the pub on the village green since the 17th century. As I made my way back to my car I caught a whiff of something good cooking and suddenly it felt like dinner time. I was soon sitting at a picnic bench in the sunny garden enjoying an alfresco lunch overlooking the village green. I ordered a Dingley Dale ham baguette served with plum tomatoes and salad. Delicious!

Deborah, the landlady told me that her steak and ale pie is a firm favourite. "We use local produce as much as we can to support local farmers and bakers. We recently opened the Vintage Tea Rooms."

I am impressed, here is a sense of community, the very lifeblood of this lovely little place.

The Cock Inn and garden

WALK 6: WALSHAM LE WILLOWS

Walsham is a Saxon name, but much earlier flint tools and sherds of Roman pottery have been found in these fields. In 1283 ninety people lived here and plenty of sheep!

1. Park the car by the Memorial Hall in the main street. There is no fee but donations are invited. Turn left to walk past The Old Stores once a grocers and drapers and the Blue Boar where Alice Pye, an ale wife, brewed and sold beer in the 14th century. It opened as a public house called The Boar in 1817 and auctions were held there.

Over the road was a house called Dages. It was built on the site of an earlier house owned by John Coggeshall, something of a rogue. He appeared in

Distance	3.4 km or 2.2 miles. A circular walk to explore the village and surrounding countryside.
Time	1¼ hours. (not allowing for lingering in St Mary's)
Start	Centre of village in the Memorial Hall Car Park in The Street
Terrain	Fairly level throughout
Map	OS Landranger 155
Refreshments	The Blue Boar serves food most day (not Mondays) from 12 noon
Toilets	In the village Memorial Hall
Getting there	Not far from the A14 or the A143. Walsham le Willows sits equi-distance between Diss, Stowmarket and Bury St Edmunds. The 338 and 304 buses run from Bury St Edmunds

court twenty-eight times for crimes such as allowing his pigs to damage crops, cutting down elms and arguing with his neighbours.

Dages, a 16th century building, was the home of a blacksmith then a wheelwright in 1817 and became a cycle shop in 1911 owned by Mr. Death. From 1911 until 1980 the jettied part of the building housed the tailor's business of Arthur Landymore.

2. Turn left by a low wall into the churchyard just before you reach Six Bells Corner where the thatched pub, named after the bells in the church, was built in 1523, originally as a house from where the Fuller family sold ale. It became a pub in 1844.

3. Crunch down the gravel path lined with elm trees and rosebushes. You reach the high roofed porch of St Mary's. Hopefully the door is unlocked. This lovely church was rebuilt in 1450 after fire damage, though the tower is one thousand years older. The nave has a fine oak roof with tie beams and hammer beams bearing the carved emblem of the 'rose en soleil', much loved by Edward IV. Behind the altar is an 1883 terracotta reredos of the Last Supper.

Inside are some old graves set in the floor, with wonderful names such as Ezekiel and Elizabeth Sparke 1779. Look too for a painting by Rosemary

Rutherford called, 'Christ Walking on The Water' (1943). The setting isn't Gennesareth in Israel, as you'd expect, but the river Thames compete with barges. Can you find the multi-coloured window with the barefoot lady? There is a link! If you have time look for the wooden plaque to Mary Boyce who, it is thought, died at the age of twenty from a broken heart in 1685.

Church of St Mary's

4. Outside by the War Memorial turn left through a gateway onto the pavement and begin to walk away from the centre of the village. You will pass Church Farm on the right. This was built in 1530, the home of Walter Martin, village blacksmith. Look out for the Priory Room on your left which bears a carved inscription; 'Suffer little children to come unto Me'.

This was built by the Martineau family as a Sunday school. It also served as a rest room for priests from Ixworth Priory. Further along the road are two sets of gabled mock Jacobean cottages with tall octagonal chimneys across the road. One reads. 'East to West – Home is Best.' These too were built by John Martineau for workers on his estate in the late 19th century providing half an acre of garden, a pigsty, a walnut and apple tree and a shared bake house and well with a pump!

5. You are walking along The Causeway beside a hedge-line which hides the parkland of The Grove with its fine specimen trees spaced apart. The house of white bricks with a domed roof (which is not visible from this point) was built by Samuel Golding a rich solicitor in the early 19th century.

6. When you see The Rectory turn left, by the triangle of grass where once four ash trees stood, taking the road to Finningham. This is Palmer Street. A few steps along brings you to Crownland Road where you bear right. Here is 16th century Clipper Cottage under its mossy thatch. Look out for the Old Bakehouse too.

The garden had apple trees laden with red fruit and a walnut tree with clusters of nuts.

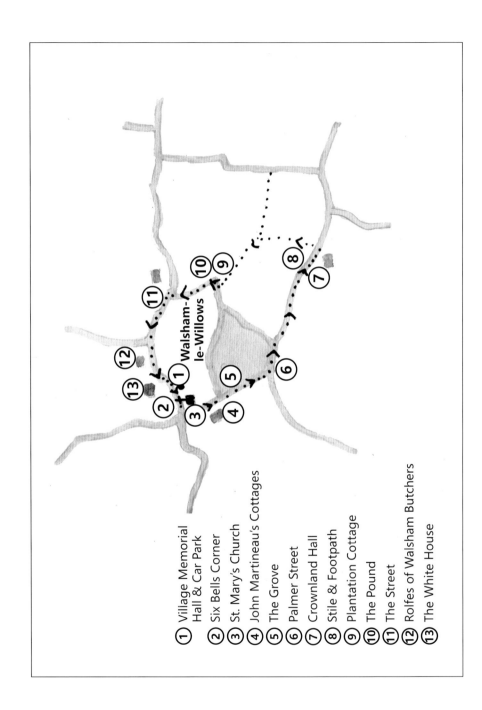

1. Village Memorial Hall & Car Park
2. Six Bells Corner
3. St. Mary's Church
4. John Martineau's Cottages
5. The Grove
6. Palmer Street
7. Crownland Hall
8. Stile & Footpath
9. Plantation Cottage
10. The Pound
11. The Street
12. Rolfes of Walsham Butchers
13. The White House

Walsham-le-Willows

Follow the road by a neatly trimmed hedge until you come to Crownland Cottage on the right. Here is more fruit – this time greengages! Next comes Crownland House followed by Miller's House on the left. Then you enter open countryside. The clay soil here is heavy and once these fields were pastures. In 15th century men would dig up this clay for building – and be fined if they were caught in the act!

The stubble fields bore the dark tracks of the combiner, evidence of the recent harvest. From somewhere ahead came the grumble of a tractor at work, ploughing the field from golden to deep brown. As I get nearer I enjoy the good smell of freshly-turned soil.

7. You come to Crownland Hall (1620) a substantial moated property where a sign on the drive says 'No Lorries'. During World War II it was used as a school.

8. Keep going until you see Ashvale where fresh potatoes are for sale in late summer. Look for a high stile (and I mean high) on the other side of the road, beside a rusty pump and pale peach, pan-tiled cottage. This is where the walk takes you over the fields. There is a small paddock to your left. You reach a second stile and the footpath bears right and crosses a small footbridge then follows the hedge line beside the Mill Field, which was recorded on a map in 1086. There are good views from here and indeed a post mill stood nearby in the 16th century. The wide grassy path you walk is called Mill Lane.

In the wind rooks fluttered like black rags among the trees across the field and as I approached a pheasant exploded from the stubble and flew to safety. The land opened up all around giving a wonderful sense of space and emptiness. Above me high cirrus cloud like angel wings floated in the blue sky. On the horizon the distant pylons brought me back to earth.

9. When you reach the other side of the field turn left by a deep ditch and head back to the rooftops of Walsham le Willows. These fields have been ploughed for hundreds of years and when I walked, the newly turned furrows of smooth clods caught the light of the sun.

The path curves right and now the first houses are near. There is a high hedge on the right of field maple and hawthorn. Then you come to Plantation Cottage and a track where you bear left, then right into Townhouse Road.

The Main Street

10. Look out for The Pound. It is brick building where stray animals were kept when land was enclosed. There are few pounds left in Suffolk and this one has been recently restored. Townhouse Road takes you by a housing estate, to a T-junction.

11. Turn left here and you are back in The Street where you began. There are newly built homes and attractive brick and flint cottages along this stretch of road. You pass The Rookery on your right. A house stood here in 1283, the home of the Hawes family but the Black Death in 1349 severely depleted their numbers. The present house was constructed in 1530.

   Then you come to Clarkes of Walsham, a builders merchants since 1873 with a display of fine summer houses. The stream ripples on your left. Look for a house called Coopers, where one hundred and fifty years ago a man with another lovely name, Zechariah Meadows, made barrels for beer.

12. Soon you will see Rolfes of Walsham, the only surviving, long-established butchers shop. It is worth popping inside to see the old photographs on the walls including one with a horse and cart standing outside.

In the shop I meet Paul Hubbard who has worked here as a butcher's boy from the age of thirteen. In 2001 he bought the business. It originally opened in 1875 when animals were slaughtered behind the shop. Before electricity came to Walsham a huge chiller filled with ice kept the meat cold. Paul tells me that they cure and smoke free-range bacon bought from local farms. They make their own pies and even bake their own bread on Fridays and Saturdays.

I take a look around the jam-packed little shop. There are Chinese pork and plum kebabs and Suffolk black bacon as well as

Outside the butcher's shop

Suffolk gold cheese; pickled walnuts; chutneys; cabbages; mangos, rosy apples, free-range eggs and of course, sweeties. I watch a little girl thoughtfully choosing a tube of smarties. I buy a small crusty loaf and wish them well.

13. Outside turn right to head back to the village hall and the car park. Pass the Congregational Chapel and the old Infant school dated 1871 also built by the Martineau family. Opposite is the Old Bakery from whence Mr Kenny delivered bread and cakes in his horse and cart and people could take pies to be cooked, as not all homes had an oven. Before he lived there it served as a butchers, plumbers and glaziers shop.

Go past the bowling green and a pretty 15th century thatched cottage called 'The White House', one of the oldest properties in the village where red geraniums and hollyhocks were flowering when I walked this way, and you will be back at the Village Hall.

The White House

WALK 7: DALHAM

I stand beneath the ancient yew trees in the church of St Mary The Virgin and breathe in the beauty. Across the valley of the little River Kennet lie a patchwork of golden and green fields – and Cambridgeshire. Beneath my feet are fragments of evidence from Saxon days. I am discovering another hidden gem in the lovely county of Suffolk.

1. I leave the car near the village hall and turn right, taking the road to Gazeley. Behind flint and brick walls are pretty, thatched cottages straight from an old-fashioned chocolate box. Birdsong, sunshine; white clouds in a blue sky; gentle breeze and summer; what more could you want?

Distance	2.4 miles or 3.8 km. An easy circular walk on country lanes, across pastures and on farm tracks. Several kiss gates
Time	At a gentle pace about 1¼ hours
Start	Village hall car park in The Street
Terrain	Some slight dips and rises, but mainly level walking
Map	OS Explorer 210
Refreshments	The Affleck Arms. Check opening times and days. Weekends all day. Depden Farm Shop and Café 8.4 miles away serves hot meals from 12.00 noon
Toilets	No public toilets
Getting there	By car; 5 miles south of A14, 8 miles north of A143 on the B1058. Bus service 16 from Bury St Edmunds

2. At the junction of Church Lane you will come to a strange conical shaped construction. Moss coats the old stepped bricks. *I find out later that this is one of two surviving Suffolk Maltings Kilns built in early Victorian times (or before) and used until the 1870s. As I stand and watch, a grey pigeon flutters out from the opening beneath a wooden cap at the top.*

3. A little further on you will find a kiss gate and a sign pointing left along the Icknield Way. Cross a grassy meadow on a well-worn path under the shadowy horse chestnut trees until, at a metal fence, you reach a second kiss gate. Now you can see the church and Dalham Hall to its left.

4. *The 14th century church once had a wooden spire on its tower, until a storm in 1658 brought it crashing down. The heavy door is locked. An apologetic note from the vicar is pinned to it explaining that lead has been stolen from the roof. I had hoped to see the wall paintings within, depicting 'The Seven Deadly Sins' and 'The Seven Mercies'. Oh, well! Instead I wander around the old flint building and am glad that I did because I find treasure; some stone memorials dedicated to;*

> *John Keates, 89 and Joseph Brett.75. 1820. Labourers.*
> *'Each of these worthy men served the family of Dalham Hall, honestly, faithfully with little interruption for half a century.*

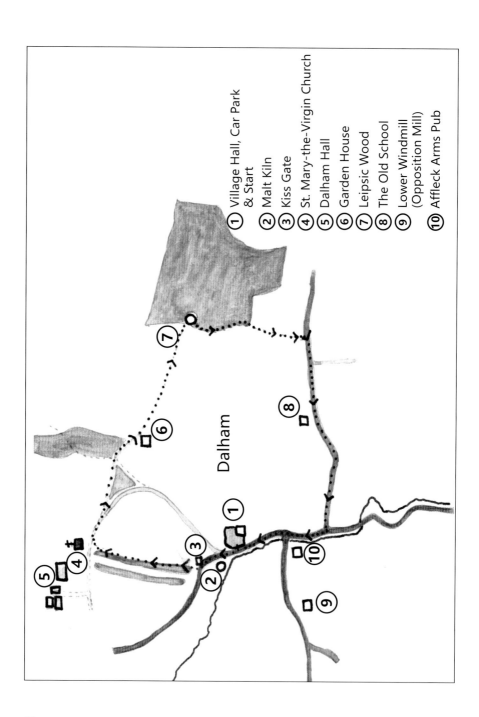

1. Village Hall, Car Park & Start
2. Malt Kiln
3. Kiss Gate
4. St. Mary-the-Virgin Church
5. Dalham Hall
6. Garden House
7. Leipsic Wood
8. The Old School
9. Lower Windmill (Opposition Mill)
10. Affleck Arms Pub

Dalham

5. From the overgrown churchyard with the headstone of Harry Death who died on 18th June 1936, you can peep over the high brick wall and see Dalham Hall itself. In the time of Edward the Confessor the manor of Dalham was owned by William the Sinner! *I wonder how he came by his name?*

A house was built here in 1313 and in 1702 Simon Patrick, Bishop of Ely, bought it for his wife and son 'to live comfortably after my decease'. (He was some twenty years older than she.) It was in need of repair so he rebuilt the house in Queen Anne style, completing it in 1705. His prediction was correct. Two years later he was dead. His good lady sold it to the Affleck family in 1714. Old pictures show it with three storeys but a fire (1955) destroyed the third floor and it never was replaced. The Affleck Arms is one of this family's legacies, as well as a huge monument by the church porch dedicated to Lieutenant General Sir James Affleck, Colonel of 16th Dragoons.

The last Affleck to own the estate married Julia Georgina Prince in 1886. She was eccentric, extravagant and also teetotal. When 'The Times' printed an article about Dalham describing it as the worst village in England with its roughnecks and drunks, she closed the pub. To the relief of the thirsty souls it was re-opened at the end of the 19th century.

Cecil Rhodes bought it in 1901 for its 'good shooting' but he didn't live there as he died in 1902. His brother built the village hall to his memory. In 1928 Laurence Philipps, a shipping magnate turned it into a stud for fine racehorses.

In 1981 Dalham Hall was sold to Sheikh Mohammed bin Rashid Al Maktoum – the ruler of Dubai. Today, neatly mowed lawns and a high wall frame the house but the sign is clear; 'Private – No Road'.

6. With the church behind you and a beautiful view of rolling fields and lush pasture, turn left and stroll down a tarmacked road. A footpath sign directs you beyond a 'Private No Road' sign and begins to ascend a little. Turn to look back for a lovely view of the church. On the right is a screen of trees hiding a quarry. You come to a wooden footpath signpost offering a choice of routes, but keep straight on into Beech Row. Look out for Garden House before you reach a T-junction. Again go straight over along a rutted track scored with tractor tyres. Through the hedge on your right you can glimpse a white windmill lower down in the valley.

View from the church gate

7. When you reach a woodland turn right where a little yellow arrow points and here the footpath dips into the trees before it re-joins the track as it approaches a narrow lane.

8. In summer the grass verge is overflowing with wild flowers. The delicate filigree of hedge bedstraw amidst white clover and agrimony with its yellow spikes all add to the beauty.

On the right you will see an abandoned red brick house set back from the road.

The paint was peeling from the windowsills and honeysuckle grew with wild abandon around the door. A painted-over sign told me that this is The Old School. Slates had slipped on the roof but I

The Old School

wondered about the memories it holds and who planted the roses that are drowning in a sea of seeding grass in what once must have been the garden?

Around the bend appears the rooftops of the village and soon you are back to The Street. You are in Denham Road. Turn right. The body of the windmill can be seen between attractive cottages.

9. The windmill was built in the 1790s. It is an octagonal smock mill and is known as The Opposition Mill as it was competing with another mill for wind some quarter a mile away! It is fifty foot high, with a beehive cap and once had four sails but a storm in 1802 blew them down.

10. Walk along The Street where the River Kennet flows alongside the road. Footbridges provide access to the houses beyond it. Look out for the Affleck Arms.

It has rolled-up parasols and hanging baskets and is open all day at the weekend – but only during evenings on Wednesday to Friday. Today is

The gentle landscape around Dalham

Tuesday and it's time for elevenses! I stop for a photo of the village sign then I am back at the car. I've been walking about one and a half hours.

Village sign

I know of a little farm shop and Café in Depden at Rookery Farm on the A143. It is some eight miles away and on my way home. Fifteen minutes later I am sitting in the garden there, surrounded by bees and flowers. This is a small holding where vegetables and soft fruit seem to be flourishing. Nearby is a noisy cockerel with a squeaky crow. If I want to learn skills such as sausage making, sheep husbandry or willow weaving this is the place to come!

I sip a Shaken Udder Milkshake and munch a fruit slice. The menu tells me that much of the ingredients used are grown here and cooked on their Aga. There's pate on toast, seasonal tarts and quiches or smoked fish platter if you're feeling hungry.

I flick through my notepad. Now where is it? Ah, here! The inscription of another memorial I found at the church. In this place of saints and sinners I'll let this humble lady have the final word.

Frances Watts.
Dairy and Poultry Woman at Dalham Hall for 29 years.
Trusty and punctual in her employments.
Devoutly attendant on the services of the church.
Diligent in reading the scriptures.
Having exemplified during a long and painful illness the patience and hope of a faithful Christian.
December 1841. Aged 72.

What an epitaph!

WALK 8: GLEMSFORD

Glemsford is one of the bigger villages in Suffolk that thrived with the 14th and 15th century wool trade when the church of St Mary the Virgin was built. Inside on the north aisle is a stone shield to John Golding who in his will ordered that the church be extended. The Goldings were a powerful family in Glemsford.

There was a settlement here as early as 1065. There are fine old houses as well as rows of cottages, which later became the homes of workers in a horsehair factory; the coconut matting industry (for coir mats and mattresses), and a silk weavers which all flourished here in the 19th century. Horsehair was used to make sofas, brushes and even violin bows! There was a thriving cottage industry and many homes housed hand looms for mat making.

Wander down Bells Lane (where the 1884 horsehair factory stood), Chequers Lane and Flax Lane (once called Workhouse Lane) to find clues to Glemsford's past. Egremont Street has some of the oldest houses in the village. The scenery around Glemsford is a hidden secret, with rolling hills and deep valleys to be explored, as well as far-reaching beautiful views.

Look out for The Angel, a 16th century *Village sign*
pub, once the home of the Golding family who funded the building of the church, and later John Cavendish, the secretary to Cardinal Wolsey. It has a 15th century carved corner post

Distance	2.5 miles or 4 km. A circular walk following field boundaries and along narrow lanes
Time	About 1½ hours at gentle pace
Start	Park in the village on a street near the village hall
Terrain	Mainly level but some gentle hills
Map	OS Explorer 196
Refreshments	Take-away snacks at Hunts Hill Stores
Toilets	Sorry. No public toilets
Getting there	No railway. Buses; The 236 Sudbury to Haverhill and the 374 Bury St Edmunds to Clare. By car leave the A1092 (a roman road) about six miles from Sudbury going towards Clare. Drive up Skates Hill off the B1065 and keep going through the Egrement Street to the far side of the village

1. Park on the street near the village hall and head towards a stretch of grass called Tye Green. Here you will see the village sign. This is where Bill Martin grazed his six cows in the 1930s (guarded from straying by a collie dog). Every evening he walked them back to Bush Farm in Shepherd's Lane to

be milked and every morning he delivered milk to the village. A public meeting was held here in 1900, when mat-weavers complained about low wages and poor working conditions. Once this was called Tenter Meadow because cloth was stretched out here to dry on tenter-hooks!

2. Overlooking the green with the village sign is Peverells – a lovely 15th century timber-framed house with mullioned windows. The Peverells manor was listed in the Domesday Book. It had thirty acres then and belonged to Ranulf Peverell. Follow the lane to your left where behind a screen of yew trees you can glimpse Coldhams – the former Victorian rectory from whence came the springtime drone of a mower when I walked this way. Above me rooks, building their nests, cawed noisily in the tall trees.

Peverels

3. Look out for a footpath to the right that takes you into the field and along the boundary hedge.

Here I met Mr. Bloomfield who has lived in nearby Clockhouse Farm for thirty years. He told me that Roman bricks and a lantern have been found in the field where we walk.

The footpath takes you across a field, to a hedge on the left and then a wooden plank bridge over a ditch towards a country road – New Street. Here you turn right and walk between fields bordered by neatly clipped hedges where chaffinchs sing their 'chiri-chiri-cheeps'.

4. Soon you will see New Street Farm across the field but here you must bear right into Plum Street. Now you can begin to enjoy the stunning views over wide-open fields that dip and rise to meet the blue sky.

5. You come to Millhill Cottage where, in Spring purple periwinkles climb a trellis up the pink wall. After a red-brick cottage bear left to Millhill Farm. Look out for clumps of pale yellow primroses growing in the grass verge by the buttressed flint wall.

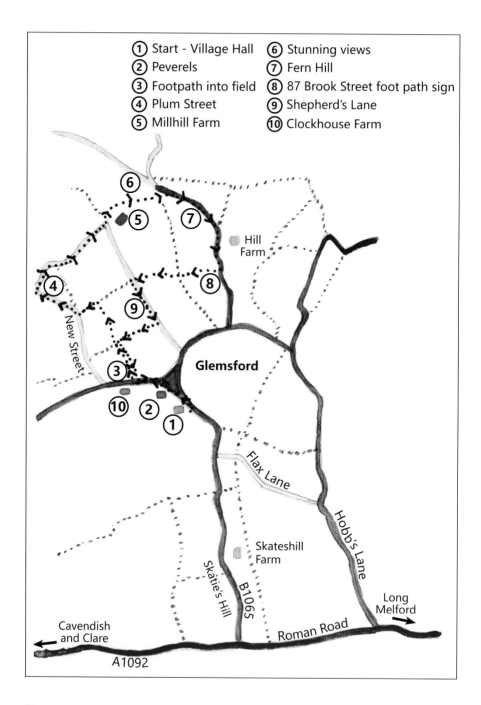

① Start - Village Hall ⑥ Stunning views
② Peverels   ⑦ Fern Hill
③ Footpath into field ⑧ 87 Brook Street foot path sign
④ Plum Street   ⑨ Shepherd's Lane
⑤ Millhill Farm   ⑩ Clockhouse Farm

On 31st May 1916 Walter Oakley, aged 11, and Robert Bloomfield, aged 10, stole two hen's eggs here. The case went to court and the police were authorised to give each lad four strokes of the birch rod, or watch as their fathers administered the punishment. The eggs were valued at 2d each.

The path led through the farm yard, past a barn with pan-tiled roof. It was brimming with discarded tyres, bits of pipe, a forgotten bicycle and stacks of wooden planks – all enhanced by the greasy smell of the diesel tank.

6. Look for an old stile beside an overgrown gateway and here you walk into pasture land where the land simply falls away before you. Allow your eyes to scan the valley and hillside as you pause to soak up the beauty.

I noticed that on faraway fields a tractor's wheels had scored a pattern of parallel lines across the pale, new green wheat and in the distance I could make out Boxford Church. It was breathtakingly beautiful. I simply stood and stared. Deep below me was a thatched roof and in the distance a tiny red post van wended its way up Braggon Hill.

7. Soon you will reach a stile where a narrow, muddy track, which can be slippery after rain, takes you to a road called Fern Hill. Here you bear right. Again enjoy the views as you walk. You come to Hill Farm where in Spring you will see a mass of purple crocuses in the garden. Now more houses appear and you are almost back to the village.

8. By number 87 Brook Street you will see a footpath on the right that squeezes between a hedge and a fence.

When I walked builders were busy here, the sound of cheerful music throbbing from their radio.

9. This is where the village is developing for you come to an estate of new houses to the left. Walk behind their neat gardens with sheds and covered benches awaiting warmer weather. Follow the path up the field edge to some tree-root steps that take you onto Shepherd's Lane, another narrow, quiet road. Here if you stop to look back you can see for miles – right to Stanstead church.

Turn left to walk down toward the village. You come to a stand which were bearing jars of white onions pickled in brown vinegar and plastic punnets of parsnips for sale. You have arrived at the allotments.

10. *A man emerged from a shed, hopeful for a sale. Alas I only had 20p in my pocket. But we enjoyed conversation which costs nothing. He told me that his name was George Shinn – one of eight children born to Sid Shinn in a two-up-two-down in Glemsford. He said that his great grandfather took part in the 1885 riot.*

The local men wanted their own polling station in the village for they had to walk to Long Melford to cast their vote and Long Melford folk were mainly Tory. Not only that, it cost them a day's wages as their employers refused to pay if they were not on the fields. Hence their anger grew as they marched and the Melford men got wind of their coming. A fight broke out, stones were thrown and windows smashed in the houses where a Tory sign was displayed.

The police, out-numbered and unsure of how to respond, sent to Bury for reinforcements and soldiers in red uniforms were hurriedly dispatched by train. As they marched up Hall Street, with bayonets fixed, calm was restored.

Keep heading down the road and ignore the first footpath to your right, but take the second which is marked, for it leads across the fields and soon you will find yourself back to the starting place – the little road by Clockhouse Farm. Turn left and retrace your steps past Coldhams to Tye Green and the village hall where this walk began.

Fern Hill

There is a public house nearby, The Black Lion (along Lion road) where food is served. Alternatively you can drive back down the street to find Hunts Hill Stores for take away tea, coffee and hot chocolate as well as snacks to keep you going. Another option, if you're feeling exotic is to visit Wongs Cherry Tree Chinese Takeaway.

You may also like to see St Mary's church a fine perpendicular building of mainly flint. It has a 14th century tower.

Overnight accommodation can be had at the 17th century Cock Inn, who offer B and B. There are plenty of other lovely walks, all clearly signposted so you may wish to linger.

Finally, Glemsford surprised me for two reasons. Firstly the beauty of the surrounding countryside and secondly the friendliness of the people I met. So when you go there – allow plenty of time to talk as well as walk. Although I do not visit the church as part of this walk, if you have time do pop inside.

WALK 9: LINDSEY

One morning in high summer when an unseen hand had painted the trees a dull monotone green and scrawled untidy seeding grass along the verges of the country road, I drove in search of a castle site, there on my map. I was heading for Lindsey.

1. Park near the church and the village hall by the road junction.

    Armed with notebook, map and camera I set off towards Groton along a quiet lane where oak trees punctuated the hedge line between me and stretching fields of golden standing wheat.

Distance	2.5 miles or 4 km. A circular walk mainly on country lanes including a visit to an ancient chapel
Time	Just over an hour
Start	Car park beside village hall. Look for the simple cross map sign on the map and there is the village hall – with a small car park. Take the road to Groton
Terrain	Fairly level
Map	OS Explorer 196
Refreshments	Nowhere in Lindsey but a short drive brings you to Lindsey Tye where The Red Rose serves food and drink
Toilets	No public toilets
Getting there	By car leave the A1071 between Boxford and Hadleigh that takes you to Kersey. Lindsey is the next village on. There are other more adventurous routes across country or you can drop down from the B1115. Buses run from Bury St Edmunds but you will need to transfer at Gedding to a 'Connecting Communities' bus – which has to be booked

2. Soon you will see Cob Cottage with windows peeping from the thatched roof and a lantern over the door.

On the left a sign points to a much restored Chapel Barn then you come to the apricot coloured farm house of Rose Green Farm hidden behind a thick screen of maple and hawthorn and towering trees. A red post box announces that; Last Collection Today is at 3.30.

3. At a crossroads turn left by White Rose House where in summer purple buddleia is alive with bees and butterflies.

I wondered if this was once a pub. I had heard that there used to be two pubs in Lindsey – The White Rose and the Red Rose. In the garden was a eucalyptus tree with

White Rose House

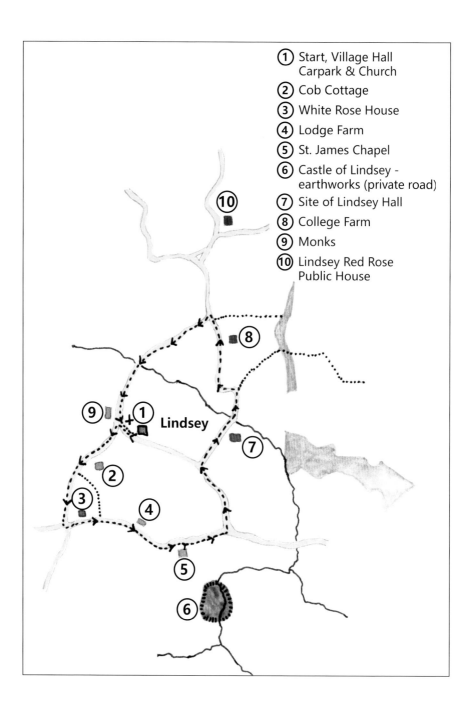

1. Start, Village Hall Carpark & Church
2. Cob Cottage
3. White Rose House
4. Lodge Farm
5. St. James Chapel
6. Castle of Lindsey - earthworks (private road)
7. Site of Lindsey Hall
8. College Farm
9. Monks
10. Lindsey Red Rose Public House

Lindsey

strange flaking bark, and behind the neatly clipped hedge were roses in full flower, a shower of discarded petals littering the lawn. Further along the road a gap to my right revealed rolling fields and clumps of woodland. Above my head the trees linked branches to create a shadowy green tunnel interspersed with bright pools of sunlight.

4. Soon Lodge Farm appears on your left. The sign says it is Leaf Mark Certified. (Linking Environment and Farming – intent on achieving a sustainable future.) Here you can buy punnets of strawberries when in season, jars of jam and other produce just inside the gate. There is an interesting weather vane on a barn.

5. A few steps on brings you to St James's Chapel – a flint building with a thatched roof that served as a barn until the 1930s when it was restored to its former use. An information board tells interested passers-by about the chantry priest who was employed to pray for the souls of the founder and his family. It was built to serve the nearby castle in the reign of Stephen and is believed to be 11th century or even older. English Heritage maintain it and it is open daily from 10am to 4pm. Free admission – but donations welcomed.

I followed the brown sign which took me on a leaf strewn path between fences to the back of the chapel where I found an old arched doorway. I stepped into the dimness where pinpricks of light penetrated the roof and dusty cobwebs draped themselves across the lancet windows. A sense of stillness permeates this humble place, with its earthen floor, simple bamboo cross and a prayer to read aloud calling back memories across the centuries. The Piscina (rounded bowls cut into the stone work) is thought to be original. I wondered about the priests who washed the sacred vessels in this very place.

6. Now you are close to the site of the castle. It is an earthworks some half a mile to the south east. But alas, I read in the chapel that it is on private land – used for rearing pheasants, and visitors are not welcomed – however curious they might be!

Oh well! I peered hopefully over the fields to where it is hidden among woodland – out of sight.

At a junction turn left along a by road – one of those leafy lanes where moss grows in the middle of the narrow road. It climbs steadily until you reach another junction by a farm, where a weeping beech trailed its branches. Here you bear right.

Now the road was edged with bracken and I saw a field where wheelbarrows stood ready by the ends of rows of runner beans that curled up tall wigwams of sticks. Someone will be coming to pick them soon.

7. The road drops down to a stream between fields edged with bracken. The site of Lindsey Hall is on your left. It stood here until 1880 when it was dismantled and shipped off to an unknown destination in America. Look out for a barn conversion.

Follow the lane upwards out of the valley and see how the landscape opens up around you.

A Muntjac deer bounded across the field, his white tail flicking. Then a land-rover approached me and the driver leaned out, asking if I needed directions. I found myself in conversation with Clive Arthey a local farmer, belonging to an established Lindsey family. It is he who told me about Lindsey Hall for he lives in its converted barn. I had read of the name Arthey in my research of Lindsey.

"Yes", he assures me, "there are plenty of Artheys buried in the church yard". Clive tells me that he has traced his ancestors back to the 1580s.

The road curved and climbed and soon a lovely view of the church could be seen above the sulphur yellow ragwort in the meadowland. The sound of vibration gave away unseen crickets in the tall grass of the verge and nearby a croaky cockerel announced his presence at College Farm.

8. You will pass College Farm on your right before you turn left towards Groton again as you reach the highest point of this pretty little road. Take time to enjoy the views before you take the downward slope back to the village.

Clouds of purple knapweed

Above clouds of purple knapweed in the bank the houses of the village and church made a lovely photograph. The road fell away to a pretty thatched cottage where pink hollyhocks looked over the wall. (On the pale blue front door the letter box is in an unusual place!)

You are almost back to the starting place, but first the road climbs steeply between high hedges and brings you to Hill Farm with its old barn swathed in pink roses.

9. To your right you will see Monks (another thatched house). Then bear left to find the church and the village hall again.

In the garden of Monks a man was clipping borders. I asked him about the name of his house. He said it was a mystery! But went on to tell me that it was built in 1584 and was once four tiny cottages. The middle section, the older part, has thicker beams and higher ceilings so was more prestigious. Indeed it was the registration office for the wool trade.

My final stop was the Norman church itself with not much of a tower and concreted walls. Inside the surprisingly large porch I found the door locked.

Almost back to the start

The Norman church

But the gravestones yielded their treasure! Phillip, Martha, John, Edith, William ... The Arthey list grows ever longer.

I never did see my castle, but I learned that it had been abandoned by the end of the 13th century. Never mind. It led me to explore yet another lovely place in rural Suffolk.

10. Before I came home I drove to the Lindsey Red Rose. It is a 15th century hall house. It serves food between 12.00-2.30pm as well as from 6.00-9.00pm. Outside are picnic benches and there is also a garden. Local beer from Southwold is on sale here.

WALK 10: CHELSWORTH

The whole of this lovely little village is in a conservation area of beautiful countryside with many listed buildings. It is about ten miles from Sudbury and ten miles from Stowmarket on the B1115.

This is a fairly easy route, across fields and along country lanes with several kiss gates for the romantically inclined! In places it follows the course of the winding River Brett, so the water meadows are sometimes flooded or muddy after heavy rain, so you may need good, sturdy boots.

Distance	2.5 miles or 4 km
Time	About 1½ hours
Start	Park in lay-by opposite The Peacock Inn
Terrain	Some gradual climbs
Map	OS Explorer 155
Refreshments	The Peacock Inn serves a lunch time menu from 12 noon and evening meals after 6 pm on weekdays. Sunday offers lunch from 12 noon. B & B is available here too. Morning coffee is available at Corncraft at nearby Monks Eleigh with hot meals here from 11am-4pm
Toilets	No public toilets
Getting there	No railway. Buses, the 753 runs from Sudbury but you need to change at Lavenham to the pre-booked Connecting Communities bus. By car take the B1115

1. Drive into the centre of the village to find the Peacock Inn and park in a lay-by under a huge London plane tree.

I chose a day in early spring, where an extravagance of elegant white narcissi flowered by old iron railings. Rooks cawed noisily in the trees that edged the course of the river, as the postman stopped to empty the little post-box by the pub then climbed back into his red van and disappeared along the road.

The Peacock Inn

2. Cross the humped-back bridges taking the road towards Lindsey. Robert Pocklington rebuilt the bridge in 1754. If you lean over you can just make out a carved stone bearing his initials. Look out for mallards and marsh marigolds in the gently flowing water below.

3. Follow the road past Bridge House, on your left and take a narrow footpath behind it, Also on the left, dandelions and plantain jostle for space with white

dead nettles, cow parsley, daisies and groundsel. You will see a farmyard on your right and paddocks with horses as you reach a kiss gate. Follow the footpath across a field where the river meanders on your left. These water meadows are littered with sheep dung – where gingery-yellow dung flies gather for romance! Hmmm! There may be muddy patches after heavy rain.

Sheep eyed me nervously as I came near and black-faced lambs with wagging tails nudged their mothers for milk. The hedge-line to my right was adorned with hawthorn flowers.

The long meadow narrows to a gateway and re-joins the curve of the river. As there is no stile, take care to shut the gate before you wander across another pasture. Look for an old willow tree that straddles the river, daring the adventurous to climb it. In the late summer you may see shimmering dragonflies and damselflies darting over the water. I am told too that the blue flashing wings of kingfishers are sometimes spotted here.

River and whispering reed beds

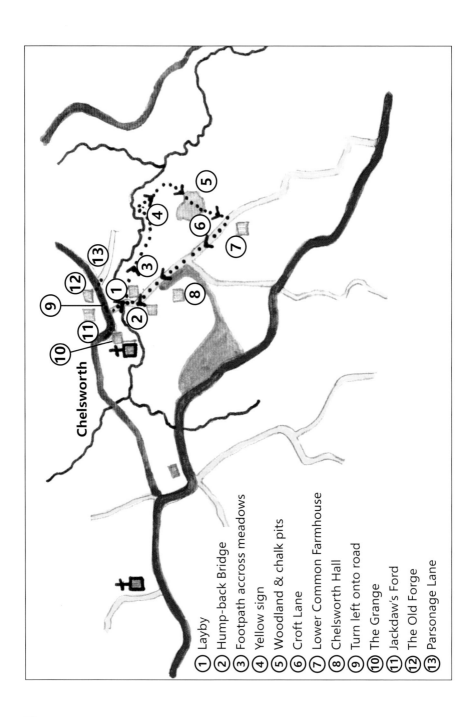

① Layby
② Hump-back Bridge
③ Footpath accross meadows
④ Yellow sign
⑤ Woodland & chalk pits
⑥ Croft Lane
⑦ Lower Common Farmhouse
⑧ Chelsworth Hall
⑨ Turn left onto road
⑩ The Grange
⑪ Jackdaw's Ford
⑫ The Old Forge
⑬ Parsonage Lane

On the far bank was a pink cottage with a red tiled roof and a big barn, and a huge stretch of reed beds where the wind whispered endlessly. Distant fields rose to the far horizon, where the florescence of first oil seed rape flowers loudly proclaimed their presence and white blossomed hedgerows appeared smudged as with smoke. The sound of a weir filled my ears – Nedging Mill on the left, half hidden by spring-green willow trees.

4. The footpath takes you away from the river and back across the field to a fence and a gate post with a yellow sign. Tramp up the grassy slopes of a meadow to woodland ahead but keep pausing to turn and look back to enjoy the lovely view of the river valley.

5. When you come to the woodland, in spring you will see dog's mercury creating a dark green carpet of poison. Yellow stars of celandines edge the pathway. There are deep pits gouged out of the ground, where chalk was once extracted. Tangled honeysuckle vines create a scene from an old Tarzan movie where the path becomes steep as it weaves through trees strangled with thick cords of ivy.

As I left the shadows of the trees and felt the warmth of the sunshine from somewhere high above me, I heard the mewing call of a buzzard.

6. A path sunken between two hedgerows (Croft Lane on the map) takes you through fields.

The day I walked this way it was dry, but with rain this could be a slippery, muddy walk. I saw that someone had ruthlessly hacked back the hedge leaving frayed branches on either side. Hopefully it will recover!

7. You will see a beige-coloured cottage with gables and dormer windows ahead of you as suddenly the road appears. You have come to Lower Common Farmhouse and what a view from here! The green pastures (dotted with tiny white sheep) dip down to the river then rise up to the faraway horizon and the wide open Suffolk sky. There is a pretty garden with a lilac tree where bird feeders sway in the wind.

Turn right to go back to the village. This quiet road is edged with grass verges where dainty yellow cowslips and white stitchwort grow. You will pass a signpost to Lindsey and Boxted.

8. Now, on the left dark shadows of yew trees hide Chelsworth, but a break for horse jumps provide an open space where you can glimpse the house. The road drops steeply taking you down to Bridge Farm with its slatted barns. When you pass Gardener's Cottage (a converted farm building on your left), you may be able to buy a box of brown mottled quail's eggs.

9. Go back over the bridge then turn left at the road, in order to see the Grange and the old church. Pretty thatched cottages line the busy road.

10. The gateway to the cemented church is near the Grange which was built in the 1400s by a rich wool merchant. It was used as a Maltings in 1550.

The Old Forge Cottage

Crunch along the drive into the churchyard. In the church is a list of vicars since 1199 and an ancient font. Take time to linger.

11. Stroll back to the centre of the village. Note Jackdaws Ford for it was once a post office and a butcher's shop. It was also the home of the Gage family, many of whom are buried in the churchyard. Mary Peacock married George Gage and had eleven children. The 14th century inn is named after her. It also served as a shop until 1977.

12. Further along the street, near to The Old Forge (a picturesque, old timbered cottage, much painted by artists) is Victory Hall, a First World War army hut. Near to thatched Chestnut Cottage with bright yellow tulips in spring, is Parsonage Lane which leads to a barn – the only remains of Parsonage House demolished over two hundred years ago.

13. A short stroll back along the road takes you to your car.

When I did the walk the Peacock Inn was closed so I drove along the B1115 to nearby Monks Eleigh for much needed refreshments and a comfort stop! The route out of the village took me past the red bricked Old School House on a sharp bend and I spotted Woodstock Cottage which in 1922 was the hiding place for silver stolen from Chelsworth Hall. I read that careless talk over a pint in the pub disclosed this secret.

Just before you reach Monks Eleigh you come to the A1141. Here you will see a brown sign pointing left to Corncraft – a popular little café where hot meals are available between eleven and four o'clock. When I did this walk I stopped here and treated myself to a generously buttered fruit scone and hot chocolate, served in a tall glass. The Ploughman's Lunch offers a choice of cheddar, stilton or ham accompanied by chunky bread from Lavenham. There is a special menu for children too. I recommend it as a fitting end of a lovely morning.

Walk 11: Bildeston

Bildeston was here when the Domesday Book was written. The site of the church marks the original village which moved down into the Brett Valley for a better water supply and to hold a market on the busier road. In the 15th and 16th centuries Bildeston flourished with the cloth trade and the timbered cottages in Chapel Street and Duke Street were once the homes of weavers, spinners and dyers.

This is a short walk to explore the surrounding countryside which mainly follows field boundaries. Be prepared for stiles and kiss gates! Upon return to the village itself you could extend your walk to the church of Mary Magdalen some half a mile outside the village. The Manor House that stood near the church was demolished in the late 1700s.

Distance	Approximately 2.6 miles or 4.2 km
Time	About 1½ hours
Start	Small car park in centre of village with its clock tower
Terrain	Gentle rise and fall
Map	OS Landranger 155
Refreshments	Kings Head Public House and Bildeston Crown which serves sandwiches at lunch time and afternoon tea (on request). For a picnic try Bank House Store where you can buy take-away food
Toilets	No public toilets
Getting there	Chambers Bus Service numbers 379, 461 and 462. By car from A1141 take the B1115. Bildeston is not far from Hadleigh, Sudbury or Ipswich

It was one of those mornings in June. Midsummer. When you are woken early by the birdsong and you catch the scent of roses as you wander down the garden to let out the hens. The sort of morning to say (as Mole of 'Wind in the Willows' said); "Hang spring-cleaning!"

So I ignored the dust and washing up and drove over to Bildeston in Suffolk   *Cottages overlooking the car park*
and parked my car by the war memorial. Armed with a footpath map and camera, I set off to explore the surrounding countryside.

1. Park in the middle of this little village, near the clock tower. Turn left and cross the road. Just beyond the King's Head (with its own brewery), you will come upon the road to Wattisham. There are pretty cottages here.

2. Turn right and keep your eyes open for a footpath on the right, by the side of house number 12. It tracks behind fences that hide gardens from curious walkers and then reaches a fork where you turn left along a shadowy, well-trodden path.

A squirrel scampered up a tree where an unseen blackbird sang its jewelled notes and brambles reached out to snag my jumper.

3. Climb over a stile. You will come to a wooden footbridge, then before you the wide landscape opens up. Follow the curve of the field boundary. Soon you'll reach another footbridge.

In summer buttercups and seeding grasses, cow mumble with swollen buds and pure white stitchwort (shirt-buttons) adorned the verge. Into the sunlit path a young hare casually lolloped. He stopped to

The clock tower

stare at me before jumping back into the oil seed rape. Then it was nothing but green fields lined with leafy hedges and the blue sky. Startled pigeons clattered from a tree and swooped away to the horizon.

The path follows the rising curve of the field and soon gives you a choice of direction. Bear left.

It was then I noticed the low humming sound of the helicopter and remembered the nearby Wattisham American Air Base. From a copse came the pungent smell of rabbits. The map indicated that this was once a roman road.

A rabbit hopped across my path

4. Soon you reach a country lane where you turn right and walk uphill to find
& a footpath to take you back to Bildeston. (There are no pavements here,
5. but little traffic.)

6. Cross the road when you see a footpath sign appear on the left pointing
   down a field.

Here there was no sign of habitation, no pylons, no rooftops – simply gentle
Suffolk farmland – nothing more, nothing less.The wide green path followed
a hedge line where blushing wild roses bloomed. In the tall feathery grasses,
ruffled gently by the breeze, white butterflies danced. The sun was warm. I
noticed a beautiful blue flower and stopped for a photograph. It was a
meadow crane's bill. It was one of those moments to treasure and remember
in the depth of winter.

7. Follow the curve of the field until you see new wooden posts and a brand
   new kiss gate! Faraway you can see the funny little church spire across the
   fields. (More of that later!)

Soon rooftops will appear and some allotments.

When I walked here I met an old man who stood staring intently at something
across the field. He acknowledged me as I drew near and his Jack Russell
greeted me like a long-lost friend. He nodded towards a post where a brown
swarm of bees buzzed. I would never have noticed them. We talked a little. His
name was John, John Bareham and he'd lived in Bildeston for over fifty years.
He told me of the changes, the housing developments and the helicopters.

"Them damn things, like an ol' bee droning in yer kitchen". Then he
surprised me.

"Yes I remember the Kray brothers too. They had a cottage here. Nice
enough gentlemen they were, always in smart suits, very polite. They helped
with the boy's club in Hadleigh. Then one morning my father-in-law
(carrying his bucket) was going to milk the house-cow. He walked by their
cottage and saw it was surrounded by police. He wondered what was going
on! Later, of course we found out."

The Kray brothers, Reggie and Ronnie were gangsters in the 1950s and 60s.
They ran a protection racket from a nightclub in Bethnal Green. Their

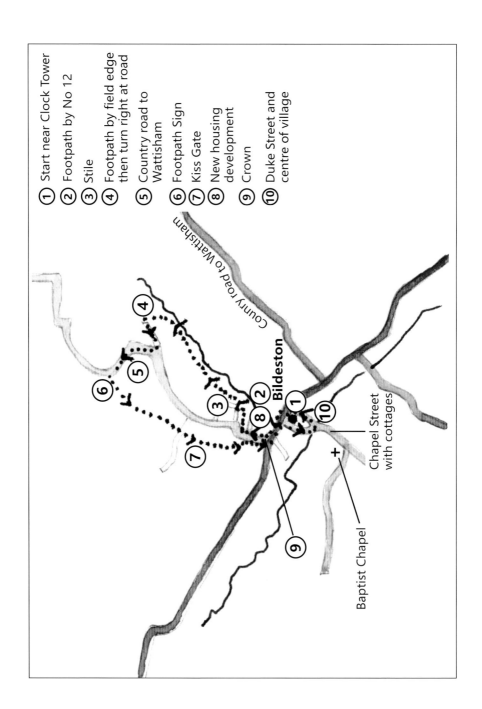

1. Start near Clock Tower
2. Footpath by No 12
3. Stile
4. Footpath by field edge then turn right at road
5. Country road to Wattisham
6. Footpath Sign
7. Kiss Gate
8. New housing development
9. Crown
10. Duke Street and centre of village

Country road to Wattisham

Bildeston

Chapel Street with cottages

Baptist Chapel

crimes included armed robbery, arson and murder. Eventually they were arrested and sentenced to life imprisonment. And Bildeston church, so the story goes, never got the £4,000 they'd promised for a new church roof!

I left John to find my way across the building site; the latest development.

8. Walk past a new housing development and find the road that leads back into the village. Turn left where you see delightful cottages on your right.

9. You will pass The Bildeston Crown, an ancient merchant's house (an inn since the 17th century). When work was hard to come by as the cloth trade demised people would seek casual employment as farm labourers and servants and The Crown became a make-do labour exchange. You will find yourself back in the Market Square surrounded by fine old houses.

Cottages on the corner

10. Take time to explore the village. At the end of Duke Street the first Baptist church of Suffolk (1737) is now housed in the 1844 building.

Wander into Chapel Street with its evidence of the thriving wool and cloth trade that once flourished here.

Back on the High street is Bank House Stores where an enterprising Mr Crickmore, the postmaster in 1871, sold groceries, ironmongery, drapes and wine as well as being the bank and the telegraph office! Today it is still busy selling snacks to workmen and running a local independent Post Office, to serve the needs of elderly folk. I buy a hot, home-made sausage roll and a cup of hot chocolate for a make-do picnic. I drive to St Mary Magdalene Church some half a mile from the village and find a sun-warmed bench where I munch – dropping flakes of pastry all over my jeans. This is such a peaceful place.

There is a curious story about this church with its strange little spiked tower. Once a village of some twenty households stood around it but the cloth trade and a market drew the villagers to the river valley. Now it is isolated. But

The weaver's cottages

on Ascension Day in 1975 some builders were repairing the tower which was unsafe. Suddenly one of them had a premonition that something awful was about to occur. The men scurried down the ladder and away from the tower as, seconds later, it collapsed in 200 tons of flint and rubble. The damage to the church roof was considerable and today we see the new tower and within, a beautiful new window depicting the two Marys.

Before I head for home and the chores that still await I take a moment to reflect as, in the quiet cemetery, I stand at the grave of two very different brothers who also lived in Bildeston – Private Arthur Welham and Private H.F. Welham aged 20 and 21. Their names are on the War Memorial. And on this beautiful day I am grateful for life and for freedom to live it well.

WALK 12: SUDBURY

At the top of the crowded market place, beyond the stalls of colourful fruit and vegetables stands a statue of Thomas Gainsborough, palette in his hand. A few steps away is the house where Gainsborough was born and once lived. But I went to Sudbury for another reason; I was intent on exploring The Common Lands (alias Water Meadows), on the edge of the Stour where Gainsborough wandered and sketched as a child.

1. Start at the Mill Hotel and crunch along a gravel path with the still waters of the mill pond and a trailing willow tree on your left until you come to a kiss gate which takes you to pastureland untouched by plough or harrow for over 900 years. Take a moment to feel the history of these ancient

Distance	2.8 miles or 4.5 km. This walk takes you across the open water meadows by the river Stour, then after a comfort stop, into the back streets of this busy market town
Time	About 1½ hours (not counting comfort stop)
Start	Near The Mill Hotel in Walnut Tree Lane
Terrain	Very flat
Map	OS Explorer 196
Refreshments	The Mill Hotel. (There are numerous cafés, take-aways and pubs in the town)
Toilets	Public toilets in Sudbury near the Town Hall and Museum
Getting there	There is a railway station nearly one mile from our starting place. Trains run on the main Norwich London line but you must change at Marks Tey. There is a bus station about half a mile away. 753 and 754 buses run from Colchester while 751 and 752 run from Bury St Edmunds. If you travel by car you can park near The Mill Hotel. There is a car park along Walnut Tree Lane

grazing lands, ditches and ponds where many native grasses, sedges and rushes thrive. In all there are 115 acres managed today by the Common Lands Charity with its 16 trustees and it officially became a county wildlife site in 2007.

Set out across the pastures following a choice of well-trodden paths with the Mill Hotel on your right. You will come to a footbridge over one of the many small ditches that criss-cross the meadows.

The wind was keen and I quickly buttoned-up my jacket. The sound of traffic lessened as I crossed a footbridge into Fullingpit Meadow. To my left a line of willows marked the river's course and to my right were the layers of grey slate rooftops of Sudbury. And everywhere there were swans, preening and tearing at grass or waddling to and from the water.

2. You will soon reach Fullingpit Weir where a roaring channel of steely Stour cascades beneath another footbridge. Cross here and walk past a concrete pill box, a reminder of the war.

A swan comes in to land on the river, its black feet stuck out amusingly for touchdown. Gulls squawk and bicker as I pass a concrete pill box stuffed with old coke cans and packaging. The cows have been taken to warm barns until next spring but the evidence of their presence remains. I take care where I walk.

3. Now the river is on your right. Keep going until you reach another bridge where in autumn and winter flag rushes stand beside dry, brown stalks of rosebay willow herb.

In the summer this is a haven for dragonflies and damsel flies; skylarks, swifts and even kingfishers but when I walked this way I met only mallards and moorhens – oh, and mole hills.

4. The path takes you between paddocks before you come to the red brick boundary wall of Brundon Hall on your right where ragged yellow leaves

A-wash with swans

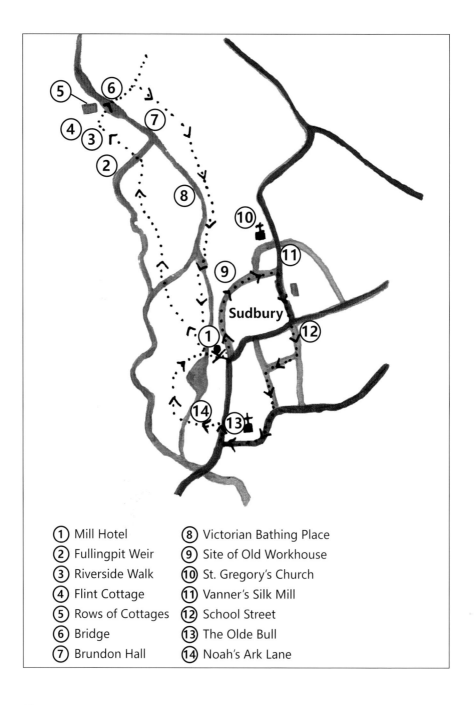

(1) Mill Hotel
(2) Fullingpit Weir
(3) Riverside Walk
(4) Flint Cottage
(5) Rows of Cottages
(6) Bridge
(7) Brundon Hall
(8) Victorian Bathing Place
(9) Site of Old Workhouse
(10) St. Gregory's Church
(11) Vanner's Silk Mill
(12) School Street
(13) The Olde Bull
(14) Noah's Ark Lane

cling to the sycamore branch that reaches out from the garden within. A low flint cottage sits on the edge of the pasture on your left. Bear to the right and you soon pass iron gates and the drive where a PRIVATE sign is nailed high in a tree.

5. Now you can see a row of pretty pink cottages with dormer windows. Beyond them turn right at the road and walk past Brundon Mill – also Suffolk pink, adorned with ivy and thick wisteria that climbs to the mossy roof.

6. There is a bridge spanning the deep mill pond which is clearly a favourite meeting place for many swans.

   Their black eyes stared hopefully in my direction as they glided, silently towards me. Here there is a gate leads to a RSPB feeding spot where kind souls can toss broken bread to these elegant birds.

7. With a woodland on your left and Sudbury ahead, turn right through yet another kiss gate (what a romantic walk this could be!) into North Meadow Common. After rain this stretch can be muddy so be prepared. Brundon Hall is now on your right half hidden behind trees. The grassland here is marshy with ditches and clumps of sedges. The Stour is to your right and the rooftops and traffic.

   After several minutes squealing children's voices could be heard until silenced by the end of playtime bell. There was clearly a school nearby. A swan flew low, straight overhead, her neck outstretched. I could hear the rhythm of her wing beats.

8. Now edging the water you will come to a low curved wall and two huge old chestnut trees. This spot marks the Victorian Bathing Place. Here many local people learned to swim before it was closed in 1937 after an outbreak of diphtheria. When you cross the bridge pause a moment to picture the bathers and to imagine the screams of the children splashing in the cold river. Follow a stony path towards the Mill (now the hotel) that has stood here for over 300 years. The old mill stream is on your left (once part of a moat around the town).

   If you are weary take a break here. Inside the picture windows overlook the Common Lands or, on a sunny day, there is a roof terrace with lovely

The Mill Pond

views. The huge mill wheel (constructed in 1889), and old photos serve as reminders of the past.

9. Once replenished leave the hotel and turn right to walk along Walnut Tree Lane. The road bends right and takes you past the old hospital site, once an austere red brick building but today transformed into the stylish apartments of St Gregory's Place.

There's something about all workhouses that both intrigues and disturbs me. This one is no exception. It was completed in 1837 - (after its faulty arches were rebuilt and its Clerk of Works was dismissed to be replaced by an illiterate successor), to house 400 inmates from Sudbury and outlying villages. Life was harsh. In January 1849 a disturbance was recorded when; 'several paupers refused to work. The ringleaders were taken before magistrates and received fourteen days in gaol.'

The 1881 census gives a long list of names - each handwritten, fastened to the page in indelible black ink; each with a story to tell. Among them; Eliza Ginn. 25. Straw Plaiter. Uriah King. 36. Silk weaver. George Edward Poll. 13. Errand boy. Abraham Rice. 79. Farm labourer (imbecile).

Lily Ambrose came to the workhouse in 1914. She was expecting an illegitimate child. Lily was fifteen. When the baby was born it was taken from her. She died in 1985. If you find her grave in Sudbury Cemetery, remember her as the woman who carried a doll all the remaining days of her life.

I recently learned that my own great grandfather, Elijah Martin died in this forsaken place. The Old Workhouse has recently been bought by developers and is currently a building site.

St Gregory's Church

10. St Gregory's church is the next stop. There is a gate in the churchyard, once the entrance to a 14th century college for priests, but as you look beyond it you get another glimpse of the converted workhouse buildings – once a sombre scene. Try to imagine sad, empty faces staring into freedom from the windows.

Inside the church is an impressive renaissance ceiling and a 15th century font cover, as well as comfortable chairs instead of pews. There is a memorial window to Capt. Robert Smylie who was killed in the battle of the Somme. He was the forty-year-old head teacher at Sudbury Grammar school who decided to enlist alongside his 'old boys'. He left a wife, three children and a pocket book with a bullet hole.

11. Outside cross the busy road which is Gregory Street to reach Vanners Silk Weaving Mill. Vanners moved to Sudbury from London in 1774 when Suffolk became a major hub for UK silk. It is deceptively large site, hidden in the middle of the town and employs over 130 people. In the Second World War Vanners wove parachute fabrics. Umbrella silk was produced until the 1980s. Today their ties are sold in Harrods and Selfridges, on Fifth Avenue and in Tokyo. They retail at £80 or more. Fabrics for furnishing and fashion are also woven and exported around the world.

12. Outside the Mill shop turn left walk along the busy one way road, passing the fire station and at the crossroads find School Street where the town's grammar school once stood. There is a blue plaque to mark the spot. Walk

by some brick terraced cottages and bear right down Straw Lane, then left into Plough Lane. Note the names that give clues to the agricultural past. You come into Church Street which takes you to All Saints Church, with its 15th century tower. Walk diagonally through the tree-lined churchyard where you can see the tomb of the Gainsborough family.

13. Back on the road turn right to pass The Olde Bull, a 16th century coaching inn where, long ago, cock fighting took place. Beyond this you come to the main road.

14. Turn right and walk a few steps along the pavement to see the narrow opening called Noah's Ark Lane across the road. Locals called it 'White Hart Lane' after the pub, now closed, to its left. It was renamed because cows were once driven here from the meadows to the dairy. It is just wide enough for the animals to walk two by two! Follow their route back to the Common Lands and on your right you will see your destination and starting place – The Mill Hotel.

As you make you way back remember that these long-established pastures have never been ploughed and many ancient species of plant, such as meadow saxifrage and sulphur clover can be found. In summer the sky is alive with incandescent dragonflies and damsel-flies, while Meadow Brown butterflies dance among the sedges where shaggy highland cattle graze and wade into the mill pond – a lovely sight.

In winter gulls squabble over scraps thrown by walkers and swans hiss at the many dogs who are walked here before they preen themselves and waddle back clumsily to the river Stour. Herons and egrets stalk along the water courses or stand as statues amidst the reeds, so do take binoculars on this lovely walk and a good coat if the weather is uncertain!

WALK 13: KERSEY

In 1252 there was weekly market in flourishing Kersey but in 1349 the Black Death claimed many lives. Wool and cloth-making helped the population to grow again until these trades moved to Yorkshire in the 17th century. Then Kersey became dependent on agriculture. But with the age of the machine and fewer farmhands required, the village community dwindled. The three shoemakers, two tailors and blacksmiths, grocer,bricklayers, carpenters, baker, saddler and draper have long gone.

This is a circular walk that explores the village and its surrounding countryside – along narrow lanes, farm tracks and fields edges, but also crossing a busy road.

Distance	2. 8 miles or 4.5 km
Time	1½ hours at a gentle pace
Start	Park somewhere in the main street by the roadside
Terrain	Some steep inclines
Map	OS Explorer 196
Refreshments	The Bell or at Kersey Mill
Toilets	In both of these places. No public toilets
Getting there	By car Kersey is close both to the A1141 and the A1071. Or catch the 84 bus from Sudbury and change at Newton to the Connecting Communities service – though you must book

1. Find a roadside space in the main street to park your car then walk to The Splash – the aptly named ford that crosses the road creating a wonderful photo opportunity. This is a good place to start this walk. Keep your eyes open for the watery theme in the names of the houses; Old River House (dated from 14th Century), Bridge House, in early summer adorned with strands of wisteria (once a bakehouse) and Water cottage. There is a horsetail dangling from the eaves of Kedges End – once the home of the 'horse doctor'. (Kedges were hand-pulled sledges once used to harvest water-cress.)

The Splash

Walk up the hill, away from the church passing Brook and Waterwell Cottages. Turn to look back at the scenic view where at the far

View up to the church

end of the street 12th century St Mary's Church rises above the red-tiled rooftops. This is a great place for photography.

The Bell Inn, with its wealth of timbered beams, is the surviving pub (1378). Here you can buy traditional home-made food every day except Monday. But I go past it heading further up the hill, which is quite steep and see more lovely old timbered houses – including the old village shop..

2. By the pump and a pretty cottage the road curves right. Take the next left turn into Priory Hill, a narrow lane leading out of the village where the site of a ruined Augustine priory is sited. This is not accessible but occasional gaps in the hedgerow afford glimpses of the rolling Suffolk farmland as the road climbs away from the village. There is a wide verge but no pavement.

    At a footpath sign on the right hand side, as you reach a bend, you leave the road to walk between fields edged by oak and field maple.

    I walked between hedgerows that promised blackberries, sloes and red rose hips. In places the path became overgrown with gangly stinging nettles and cow-mumble stalks as tall as me where brown ringlet butterflies danced. I heard the rasping screech of a Jay and saw the stripe of blue on its wing as it flew deeper into the trees.

    Take a right hand path that leads into woodland.

    The arching brambles snagged on my coat. In the pine and larch trees was the sound of unseen birds. Tall aspen trees fill the air with their noisy, hollow-stemmed rustling sound.

    Watch out for another yellow arrow sign that confirms you are still on track. Pass a huge oak, laden with acorns, near a wooden bridge.

    Soon you will see another footpath, bearing right, which leads to a well-trodden bridleway. Here is a good view of the church across the fields. Soon buildings can be seen ahead.

3. You come to farm buildings and a long-forgotten combiner where tall burdocks grow to hide old machinery, including an ancient cement mixer. This is Rushes Farm. Crunch your way along the stony drive to the

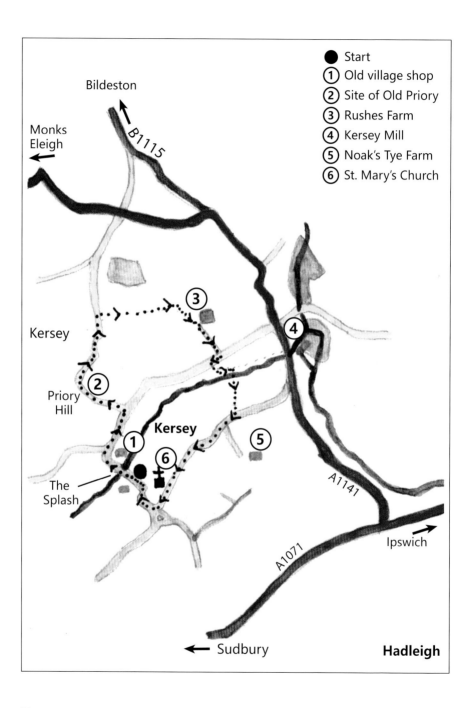

Start
① Old village shop
② Site of Old Priory
③ Rushes Farm
④ Kersey Mill
⑤ Noak's Tye Farm
⑥ St. Mary's Church

Bildeston

Monks
Eleigh

B1115

③ Rushes Farm

④

Kersey

Priory
Hill

②

Kersey

①

⑤

⑥

The
Splash

A1141

A1071

Ipswich

Sudbury

Hadleigh

tarmacked lane. Here you turn right to follow the road a short distance before you turn left by a tumbledown shed onto another footpath that crosses a field. At this point you can see the church again standing tall against the skyline. Listen out for skylarks rising from the fields, trembling in song. Bear left down the field edge and follow the stream line until it reaches a busy road – the A1141. Turn right, but take care as there is no pavement.

4. Keep to the grass verge for a short distance before you cross the road to call at Kersey Mill. Allow time to linger here and take a comfort stop.

Here I saw stunning wildlife photographs. I visited 'Little Treats' café and enjoyed a raspberry and almond cake to accompany my hot chocolate. I was told that there are plans to get the mill working again. The menu looked interesting, I decided to call back later.

5. From the entrance to the mill see the little road that climbs back to Kersey. Carefully cross the busy road again and climb steadily for about a mile up the narrow lane which leads back to the village, always heading towards the tower St Mary's Church. (If you prefer there are footpaths in the fields left and right – see the OS Map.) Look out for Noaks Farm on your left.

Church across fields

As you near the church, Rushes Farm can be seen in the valley to your right.

6. Stop to take a look inside this old country church.

At the church I pushed open the heavy door and stepped into the stillness and familiar church smell. The silence was tangible. I stood near the old parish chest to listen to the deep ticking of the clock like a heart beating away time. Information sheets told me of the headstone of John Mann somewhere in the churchyard. He was executed at Bury in 1828 for highway robbery in Hadleigh. Later I searched outside in the tall grasses, but failed to locate it. I also read of the village shop – owned by Mr. Stiff.

From the churchyard pause to enjoy the far-reaching view of the rooftops and beyond, before climbing down some steps into the road that takes you back to the village.

Rooftops from churchyard

When I walked here I also had an appointment with Mr Jack Stiff himself who has lived in Kersey for all of his 85 years. I found his house and soon was seated at his table enjoying his stories. I learned that Stone House, Collett Cottage, Pointer's Lodge and Quills were all once part of the village shop. Quills was the pork butcher department. Jack's father and uncle ran it in the 1920s, and before them his grandparents. Market house was the butcher's shop prior to this time.

"We sold everything apart from wet fish and second hand women." He chuckled. Indeed they were noted for brushes, pails, glass, earthenware, motor tyres, oils, petrol, carbide – for bicycle lamps, flour, hams and corn.

"We even sold televisions before there was electricity in Kersey. It only came in 1952", he added. Jack won a scholarship to Sudbury Grammar so was not in Kersey School when "a shell came through the roof in 1940 and hit the piano". He wanted to be a chartered accountant but "father needed me in the shop", so he started work in 1945 after his sixteenth birthday. Jack met Jill on a delivery round. They married in 1958.

He talked of Grandma Stiff, a formidable 93 year old, who checked that everywhere was locked at night, hobbling about with a broom as a walking stick until she died in 1956. No-one dared light up a cigarette in her presence – or they were in trouble!

Today Jack and Jill Stiff remain in the street where he has always lived and their son lives at Rushes Farm.

As the walk come to an end and your car awaits, if you're feeling in need of sustenance, you have a choice of eating places at either The Bell (if you've timed it right) – or driving back to the tea rooms at Kersey Mill.

WALK 14: MONKS ELEIGH

Before you begin, a little history for the name Monks Eleigh holds a clue to the past. In the 10th century the Manor of Illeigh was bequeathed to Canterbury Cathedral. For hundreds of years the Dean and Chapter of Canterbury owned the land, farms and homesteads, leasing it to tenants and providing a priest for the church which was first built in 1350. So here is the ecclesiastical link. The village prospered in the 14th and 15th centuries with the wool trade when many of the fine old houses were built. In the early 20th century there were many little shops. Two butchers, a grocer, a dealer in tea, a tailor, an egg-merchant, as well as two blacksmiths a thatcher and the inevitable undertaker.

This is a circular walk through this picturesque village and into the surrounding countryside, along country lanes, besides orchards and across fields.

Distance	2.8. miles or 4.6 km
Time	1½ hours – allowing time to linger in the church
Start	The central village green
Terrain	Gentle rise and fall
Map	OS Explorer 196
Refreshments	The Swan. 11am-3pm Tuesday to Thursday. 11am-11pm Friday and weekend. Sandwiches and apple juice in village community shop
Toilets	No public toilets – only in pub
Getting there	Monks Eleigh sits north of the A1141 between the larger towns of Lavenham and Hadleigh. Connecting Communities Buses run from Hadleigh but you must book beforehand

1. Park by the much-photographed green with its pump, village sign and lovely cottages and pause to enjoy the view before you head up the road to St Peter's church.

Before the pump (1854) villagers drank from Lavenham Brook, down in the valley and it wasn't until after the Second World War that mains water was piped to Monks Eleigh.

Cottages and church

Leave the road and crunch up the tree-lined, stony drive that leads to the old church with 15th century flints in the west doorway at the foot of the tower. Hopefully it will be unlocked as it was when I walked this way.

I pushed open the heavy door and stepped into the stillness within. I see the pulpit that has been there for five hundred years, with its carefully carved tracery of delicate flowers in the panels.

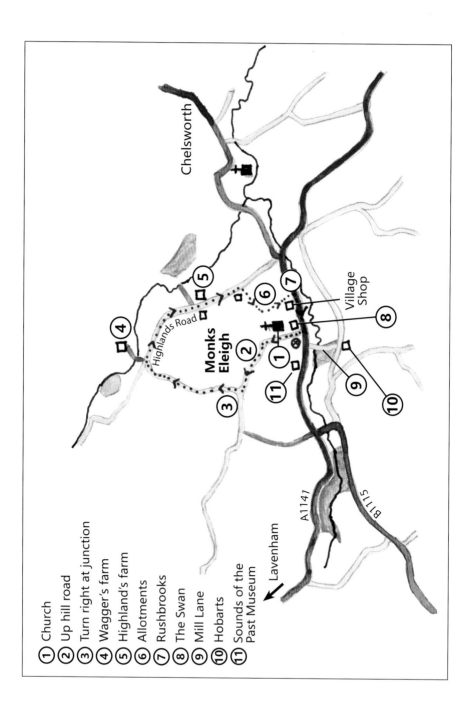

Chelsworth

Highlands Road

Monks Eleigh

Village Shop

Lavenham

A1141

B1115

① Church
② Up hill road
③ Turn right at junction
④ Wagger's farm
⑤ Highland's farm
⑥ Allotments
⑦ Rushbrooks
⑧ The Swan
⑨ Mill Lane
⑩ Hobarts
⑪ Sounds of the Past Museum

I take time to read the roll of honour – the names of twenty-two young men from this village who were killed in the First World War. One is Private Edward John Hollox, of the Suffolk Regiment, aged 18 who died in May 1915. He was once a bell ringer in this very church and there was a commemorative ring of bells to honour him in May 2015. He lived across the road at The Mill in the Causeway. I determine to find the house later.

2. Continue your walk up the hill beyond the church and you will soon leave the village behind.

   A chaffinch chirruped noisily from a hedge where wild roses bloomed. There was a good view across the wheat fields where swallows swooped and dived.

3. You will come to a junction with a central signpost. Turn right towards Kettlebaston. Look out for the spire of Bildeston church on the horizon beyond a Suffolk pink farmhouse.

4. Follow the road until you come to another junction where you turn right to pass Wagger's Farm with its organised paddocks where ponies graze.

Signpost

Here Highland's Road starts to climb steeply back towards Monks Eleigh. There is no pavement only a grass verge, but few cars pass this way.

On a day in autumn cow-mumble towers above the seeding grasses and old man's beard clings to the hedges twining among the berries.

5. At a farm workers cottage opposite Highland's Farm look out for a footpath sign that directs you to the right. It takes you beside the cottage garden then between the open fields towards The Old Rectory where pink roses climb the grey brick walls. There is a lovely sense of space here.

6. At the far side of the field turn left behind the Old Rectory and you will soon come to allotments with rows of broad beans. The church and cemetery is to your right and you will see a gate ahead. The path now leads you beside an orchard.

There was a man at work, thinning fruit. I stopped to talk and found out that his name was George Hodgkinson, a retired city shipping lawyer who planted two orchards here ten years ago. He wanted to grow apples and planted twelve varieties including St Edmund's Pippin and Ashmead's Kernel with a sharp intense flavour. The apple juice, pressed locally is for sale in the shop. He also planted six varieties of plums – one being an old Suffolk plum – Coe's Golden Drop.

7. The path meets the busy A1141 road opposite a house called Rushbrookes. Turn right on the pavement and you will come to the Community Shop.

The little shop was jam-packed with all you could ever want from potatoes to stem-ginger, newspapers to wine. I spoke to Janet the manager, who told me that the shop is run by a committee and manned by forty-five volunteers who work shifts.

"If anybody wants something I try to get hold of it. We do local eggs and bacon, raspberries and of course, local apple juice." I treat myself to three bottles.

8. Outside walk towards The Swan – a thatched pub with a good menu after 12 noon. There used to be four pubs in Monks Eleigh – The Bull, The King's Head and The Lion.

I notice they serve fish-finger sandwiches with tartar sauce or a healthier option, cheese, tomato and salad.

9. You come back to the village green but if you wish to explore further cross the busy road and find a left turning into Mill Lane. This is where you will see the home of Private Hollox, the bell ringer – the Old Mill House. The lane drops down between trees to the shallow River Brett. Cross the footbridge and follow the tarmacked footpath between tiny streams where yellow irises and turquoise blue forget-me-nots flower.

10. It comes out into Back Lane and here is Hobarts, a 15th century black and white timbered house with lattice-leaded casement windows, and a big external chimney stack. It looks as if it belongs in a children's story book. During the war (the story goes), it was used by aeroplanes as a land mark – but today the trees around it have grown tall.

Hobarts

11. Retrace your steps to the village. A few steps further along the road you will see the United Reformed church built in 1870 for Protestant Dissenters. Now it houses a museum; 'Sounds of the Past'.

My curiosity led me to peep in at the open door. The room is stacked full of old radios and gramophones. I heard movement and turned to see a man wearing a cap and a smile. He introduced himself. His name was Paul Goodchild. He has lived in Monks Eleigh for most of his seventy years.

"Me mother had a little shop opposite The Swan. She used to sell sweets and that ... and fish and chips. She used to cook it at the back of the shop. Me father used to gew to Lowestoft to git the wet fish. There were several shops in the village then; a greengrocers and two butchers. I used to get meat for me mother. At that time there was all straw on the floor because they used to slaughter the pigs at the back. I lost my father in 1953. He died of pneumonia. I was only abowt eight.

Village scene

> *I've been into old farm machinery all me life and when I retired I wanted to do something different. I'd spent hours and hours watching a man repair old radios and I developed a passion to do the same.*

> *We open the first Sunday in every month. We have live music - a man plays the Hammond organ and another a banjo. All the gramophones work. We've got a barrel organ and juke boxes and over 500 radios. Me wife does tea and cakes. Unfortunately last year I was diagnosed with cancer so I collect for Macmillan nurses. The chapel's bin empty for over twenty years. They let me have it rent free."*

Make your way back to the village green a lovely place for a picnic - with local apple juice from the community shop. Or pop into The Swan to prolong your visit to this lovely little village.

WALK 15: CHARSFIELD

There is a book called 'Akenfield' written by Ronald Blythe which was published in 1968. It paints a vivid, but realistically, ruthless portrait of life in a Suffolk village. When I read it, someone mentioned that it was based in Charsfield. The book is a record of the honest memories of the people who lived there when Ronald Blythe interviewed them. In 1974 the book became a film and has recently been re-released. Some today remember the film being made!

Charsfield sits in a valley, only 25 metres above sea level. It is farming country, nothing more, nothing less – a mix of heavy clay, light loam and sand, arable land with occasional pockets of woodland. It is three miles from Wickham Market and seven miles from Framlingham.

This is a circular walk along country lanes, through orchards and across fields.

Distance	2.9 miles or 4.7 km
Time	1½ hours
Start	Park somewhere in the middle of the village in The Street. There is a layby near the Three Horseshoes Pub
Terrain	Gentle slopes up and down
Map	OS Explorer 212
Refreshments	Tuesday Coffee Morning (recommended) in the Baptist Chapel Hall. The Three Horseshoes – a free house serving local ales and home-cooked food. Closed on Mondays
Toilets	No public toilets but facilities in both of these places
Getting there	Drive along narrow lanes to Charsfield, from the B1078 – not far from the A12 or catch the Connecting Communities bus from Framlingham – but you must book beforehand

1. Facing the pub, turn right and set off along the road, passing Well Cottage and Thimble Cottage, until you reach the Baptist chapel on your left. It is a solid red brick building under a pan-tiled roof and it invites us to 'Enter into His gates with Thanksgiving', as it has done so for two hundred years since 1808.

On the morning when I walked this way I saw a board with a notice stating;

Tuesday Coffee Morning. 10-12. All are welcome

Well, what perfect timing! It was Tuesday and 10.10. As I hesitated, a friendly voiced called, "Are you out walking, would you like a coffee?" That clinched it. It was the minister of the chapel and when he knew my purpose he introduced me to 86-year-young Cyril Kindred, a long-time resident of Charsfield.

So I found myself in the new hall of the chapel, surrounded local residents, all happy to chat – including Cyril himself. As I scribbled notes as fast as I could, Cyril talked. The youngest of eleven children he left school aged 14 and started work the next day for a grocer in Wickham Market; Albert J. Hall. "A wonderful man."

When he passed his driving test Cyril became the delivery van driver. In 1972 the business was sold to the Co-op and Cyril worked for twenty-three years as a milkman.

"There was no mains water, sewers or electricity in the villages in them days."

When the opportunity for electricity came, Cyril's landlord said he couldn't afford it.

"If you want it you'll have to pay fer it yerself." So Cyril did. In his two-up-two-down cottage (rent six shillings a week), he had four light bulbs put in, one central to each room and two thirteen amp plug sockets.

"It cost me fifteen quid!" He chuckled. Cyril told me that he's been a member of the Baptist Chapel for sixty-one years. "Are you a Christian?" he asked me. I said that I was. "See you in heaven then. I can't wait." He added.

I munched tangy lemon cake, oozing with creamy icing and sipped fresh coffee and found out that the ditch behind the hall was once the Potsford river. It brought Dutch boats with a cargo of green and blue tiles before returning with potash. I could hardly believe it. Over the years it has dried up into the tiny stream it is today.

"It was known as the Black Ditch." The minister told me. When I asked why, Cyril said it was because of the sewage!

Several people talked about the Akenfield filming in 1974. Some had relatives who were in it others remembered Ronnie Blythe who lived in nearby Debauch (Debidge). He was a regular worshipper at St Peter's Church in Charsfield.

2. Turn left at the Chapel and walk up the hill called Chapel Lane.

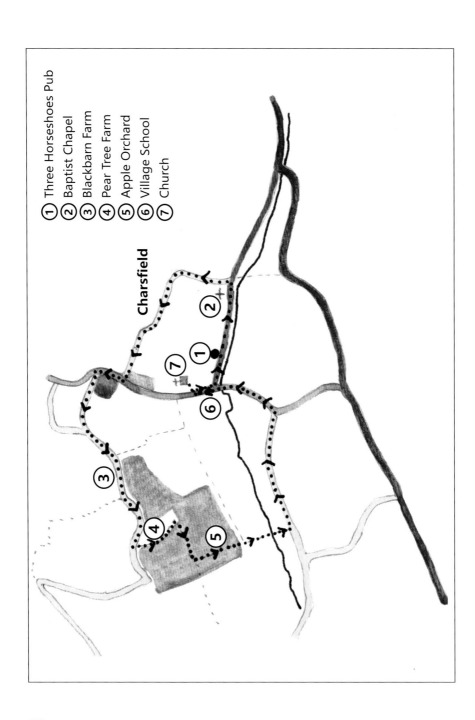

① Three Horseshoes Pub
② Baptist Chapel
③ Blackbarn Farm
④ Pear Tree Farm
⑤ Apple Orchard
⑥ Village School
⑦ Church

Charsfield

The verges were a riot of tangled vegetation; tall nettles and cow-mumble, compete with purple thistles and prickly burrs with the odd red splash of a poppy.

Look out for a gap in the hedge to see the church peeping over the fields. Pass Hilltop Cottage with a rustic arch festooned with roses. Magpie Street is on the left but you follow the road right, before taking a left hand turn.

From a cottage an elderly man was carrying his rubbish. He grinned when he saw me.

"I leave my rubbish at my neighbours, I live alone since my wife died and don't have enough to bother them stopping. I've lived here for fifty-eight years." He asks me where I come from. When I tell him near Sudbury he smiles thoughtfully. "I've heard of it..."

3. You will come to Blackbarns Farm.

4. Then comes an orchard and Pear Tree Farm with its steeply pitched roof. You will find a footpath on your left that drops down beside a field of

Church across the fields

blackcurrant bushes. In places there are openings in the tall hedge showing views across the wide fields to distant farm buildings.

As I wandered by the bushes, branches were bending with heavy clusters of shiny, black berries. It was midday and the air had become sultry. A helicopter droned overhead in a deep blue sky.

At the corner where the blackcurrant field ends, turn right and walk along the lower edge.

5. The map shows the footpath bearing left by some apple trees. Search for the sign which is well hidden in the hedge that edges the orchard, now on your right. Beyond the fruit trees a yellow arrow points straight on towards the road.

The track was wide and in the stubble field were the fat cylinders of golden bales where a man walked with his dog, beneath a clear blue sky.

As the path drops down into the valley you come to a bungalow and the road. Here you turn left.

Rolled up bales

The heat was intense. In a stable a bay horse stood motionless in the shadows. Some roofers were at work in the scorching sun.

"I should git inside if I was you, and have a gin and tonic!" one man called.

Follow the road and soon you will see the red brick tower of the church appearing above the trees. Turn left at the junction. The road takes you between the shades of high hedges, back to the village.

Cross the bridge over the Polstead River and you are back in the village.

6. Walk up the hill, passing a signpost bearing delightful names to find St. Peter's church to your right, behind a round topped wall. The 1863 village school is nearby.

From an open window in the school which stands opposite the church came the sound of children's voices singing.

Signpost to Suffolk villages

7. Take a few moments to visit the lovely old church surrounded by trees.

The English bond brick tower dates from the 15th century but there is an arched Norman window in the north wall of the Nave that gives a clue to its history. The Hammer-Beam roof is 14th century. The Pews are imports from All Saints Church in Debach. The bench ends were carved by Mr Lanman who lived in Framlingham during restoration work in the early 1900s. There is one of a pelican. Outside there is an interesting wrought iron clock high on the tower.

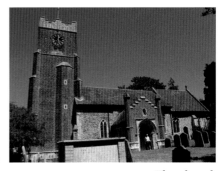

Inside it was blissfully cool. Sunlight slanted in the plain windows above the altar. From the roof carved figures forever clutching heavy books, looked

The church

down on the empty pews where quirky creatures have been carved; a squirrel and a boy in the stocks. The organ was perched high in the bell tower where a beam, once in the old parsonage is inscribed – 1585. I left Esther Eliza Gibson. Nurse to the village and Servant to the Church to the quietness, disturbed only by the chiming of the metal clock on the tower.

Retrace your steps to The Street turning right at the sign post, but stop to savour the wonderful names. Just beyond the village hall, on your left you will find the lay-by and hopefully your car! If you've timed it right the Three Horseshoes pub should be open with home-cooked food and the promise of Adnam's Ales.

Walk 16: Framlingham

This a busy market town is overshadowed by the impressive walls of an ancient 12th century castle that was built by Roger Bigod as a family home after William the Conqueror gave him the Manor of Framlingham. He became the first Earl of Norfolk. Indeed for over four hundred years the Dukes of Norfolk lived there. It is said that Mary Tudor came here to plan her proclamation as Queen of England.

This walk takes you around the castle ramparts, along field edges to higher ground for a good view of the towers and walls. Then it drops back into the town where you can explore the little lanes and small independent shops. Every Saturday and Tuesday there is still a market here.

On my first visit I drove up Church Street and parked the car near the castle beneath a tree laden with ripe apples. It costs £3 for the whole day. It was an *early, golden morning in October. In the deep blue sky rooks cawed around the castle ramparts. I walked towards the heavy castle door which was still closed, so I scrambled up and down earthworks, across the dewy grassy lower court, along the bailey ditch and thereby skirted around the whole towering stone edifice stopping only to read boards that told me snippets of history.*

'The prison tower housed obstinate men who deserved hanging'.

'If they caught a heron poaching their fish in the Mere, they would eat that too.'

Distance	3 miles or 4.8km
Time	An hour or so
Start	Car Park by Castle. £3 a day at time of writing
Terrain	Up and down, some steep banks and steps
Map	OS Explorer 212
Refreshments	Sandwiches in supermarket. Several cafés with outside seating for sunny days as well as The Crown public house which serves locally sourced food
Toilets	Public toilets in castle car park
Getting there	By car Framlingham lies between the A12 and the A1120 and is on the B1119 and B1116. 552 buses run from Diss and 555 from Debenham

1. Join me to park near the castle. Walk towards the castle gate. (If you want to look around the castle itself, today owned by English Heritage, it costs £7.60 for adults; £6.80 – concessions as I write this. The castle opens at weekends during the winter months, so check before you decide to visit. There is a wonderful walk around the castle ramparts (if you aren't too nervous of heights) which offers stunning views of the town and surrounding countryside. There is an informative exhibition within. The castle became a prison during Elizabethan times.

2. Bear left to take steps down a steep path into the dry moat. Be careful there is no handrail in places. The stone towers and ramparts with their

Tudor chimneys rise above you and to your left appears Framlingham College- an impressive turreted red-bricked mansion beyond the Mere.

When I walked here the waters of the Mere sparkled in the sunshine and white swans floated on its blueness while black cormorants flew overhead.

The present castle has only seen one battle, when it was besieged (briefly) by King John in 1216.The curtain wall has 13 mural towers. The prison tower was built in the 13th century for local poachers and religious dissidents. Mary Tudor stayed in the castle (1553) when the ornamental chimneys were added. It was here she heard the news that she had become Queen of England. The Dukes of Norfolk owned the castle for over four hundred years. Above the gatehouse you can see the Howard coat of arms.

The 1613 records tell us it was becoming derelict and Sir Robert Hitcham bought it. He demolished many castle buildings and used the bricks to build his alms houses (1654) providing homes for six local widows and six local widowers. These men were given a hat and blue coat once a year, while the women – a bonnet and gown. In 1666 when plague struck the town it became an isolation ward for infected patients.

The castle walls

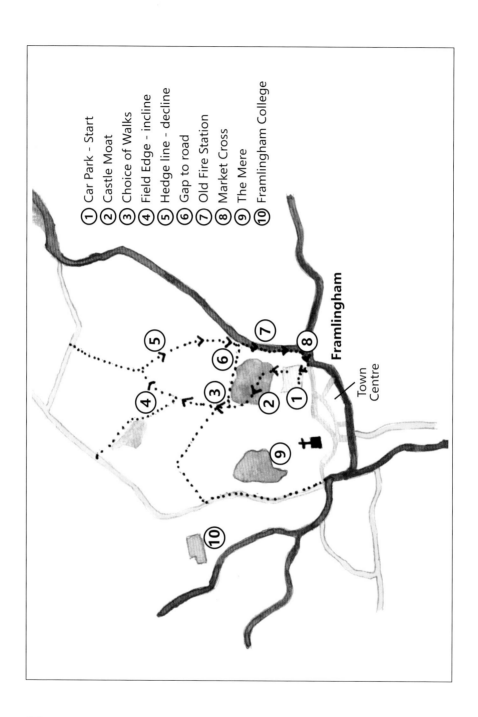

1. Car Park - Start
2. Castle Moat
3. Choice of Walks
4. Field Edge - incline
5. Hedge line - decline
6. Gap to road
7. Old Fire Station
8. Market Cross
9. The Mere
10. Framlingham College

Framlingham

Town Centre

3. Stroll across the grass where people enjoy picnics on summer days then take some steps down to a footbridge. Here is an information board about the creatures that live here and directions for a Nature Trail around the Mere. If you are a lover of wildlife you may prefer to explore this part of Framlingham. There are nearly three hundred species of plants and eighty species of birds. So take your binoculars.

4. For my walk go straight on towards a kiss gate. Look out for tree roots across the path. Follow the path edged with nettles and tall cow mumble in summer, between tall ash and oak trees, as it begins to climb. You will come to a field, bear right and keep tramping upwards with the hedge (of mainly field maple) to your right. If you look back you will see the turrets of Framlingham College, an independent school for 13-18 year olds. It was built in 1864 in memory of Prince Albert, Queen Victoria's husband.

   Bear right again, just beyond a mature oak tree and now you will see the castle itself, sitting above the trees.

5. Now follow the path down the hill, with the hedge (where red rosehips gleam in autumn) to your left.

6. You will cross a ditch on a footbridge then head up the slope towards the road. Follow the curve of the field and you will find a gap in the hedge, by a footpath sign.

7. Turn right on the pavement and make your way back into the town. Look out for the Old Fire Station, now the headquarters of the Scouts and Guides.

8. Soon you will see the Market Cross, bear right into Castle Street with its quaint houses and cottages. This brings you back to the castle and the car park.

   At this point I decided to explore the town itself.

   The market square was jam-packed with stalls and shoppers.

Street scene and church

Tables spilled out of cafés onto the raised pavement and there was an enticing smell of coffee. The Crown Hotel, a grade II listed coaching inn was built in 1554 for Mary Tudor's knights. Its courtyard was once accessible to horses and carriages through the central entrance where the stable block was found. It is said to be haunted!

The Crown

I wanted to see to the Hitcham alms houses that I'd read about at the castle. I found them in New Road and met Julie Scott, the manager, on her regular round of visits to the residents. We were soon chatting. She told me:

"I have been keeping a close eye on 'my family' for fifteen years. I listen to memories, help with form-filling and I'm always at the end of the telephone if anyone needs me. There is a waiting list and you can only live here if you are over fifty-five, have a local connection or have lived in Framlingham longer than two years. In the 1970s a small rent was introduced – before that they were free."

Not far from the Hitcham alms houses is Wells Close Square and the offices of Clarke and Simpson, chartered surveyors and auctioneers. The building they occupy was once a gentleman's outfitters. Geoffrey Clarke was a grain merchant in the early 1900s with a stand in Ipswich Market. This was how it all began. His son, Christopher became one of the founding partners of the business which deals in rural property matters including farm and land sales, lettings and estate management within Suffolk and beyond.

I found a sandwich shop nearby and armed with lunch walked back to the town centre in search for Double Street and its 1856 Victorian pillar box. Sure enough there it was on the junction of Castle Street. I also popped into St Mary's Church to find the tomb of the 3rd Duke of Norfolk.

A little later, full of Suffolk ham and cheese sandwich I went back to the car park. I scooped up a rosy apple from the tree there and navigated the one way system out of the busy little market town watched over by its castle through many centuries and still thriving today.

WALK 17: WISSINGTON

The map says Wissington. The locals say Wiston and so do the old books. So there you have it. In 1883 West Suffolk County Council decided to make Nayland and Wiston one civil parish - against the wishes of the Wiston folk but this scattered village still retains its agricultural heritage with seven working farms today.

A walk along country lanes, across fields into the hills, before joining the Stour Valley Path in the river valley.

Distance	3.5 miles or 5.6km
Time	1¾ hours
Start	Near the Nags Head Corner, on the main road – suggested parking on the edge of Nayland as close to the staggered crossroads as you can get
Terrain	Some steep slopes up and down in middle of walk
Map	OS Explorer 196
Refreshments	Some public houses in Nayland including The Anchor, in Court Street, open daily – also offers a take-away menu
Toilets	No public toilets on walk
Getting there	Take the A134 from Sudbury to Colchester or find a cross country route from Bures

Park your car on the edge of Nayland – not far from Nags Corner. There is a safe place to cross the busy A134 which leads you to Wiston Road. Here the walk begins with houses strung out along the roadside on your right and a barbed wire fence to your left.

The few houses are soon left behind. Glossy black cows graze behind a barbed wire fence. A noisy tractor is busy spearing bales and loading them onto a trailer, in a field of yellow stubble. Tired looking nettles and dried grasses edge the road.

1. After the last house you come to a footpath sign. It points right beside a laurel hedge along a narrow path that climbs steadily upwards between rough grazing land and a woodland or hedges.

   There are rolled up bales of hay in a meadow to my left. I duck under branches laden with elderberries and pluck a bramble that has snagged my jumper. Now from an old oak a grey pigeon flaps across

Wiston church

124

my path. A small stream trickles beneath a footbridge. A timbered house becomes visible beyond a hedge where fat blackberries gleam. The path becomes overgrown here, with whirls of cow mumble seed heads, higher than me.

Beyond the curve of the hillside is another house – Smokey Farm, its windows peeping down across the valley.

2. The track bears left but a yellow arrow sign points walkers to the right at two gateways before squeezing between fences. In summer pale blue scabious and crowned ribwort plantain decorate the path until it comes to a lane. Smoky Cottage stands here with clumps of purple lavender in the garden.

3. Turn left into Campion Lane, a narrow, stick-strewn road where elm trees cast their shadows. Soon you see the farmyard of Hill Farm with an assortment of barns and outbuildings where various cars are assembled.

4. The road curves past the red brick farmhouse itself and drops down the hill. You pass Sandpits Farm. Ignore a footpath to your right. Gaps in the

The surrounding countryside

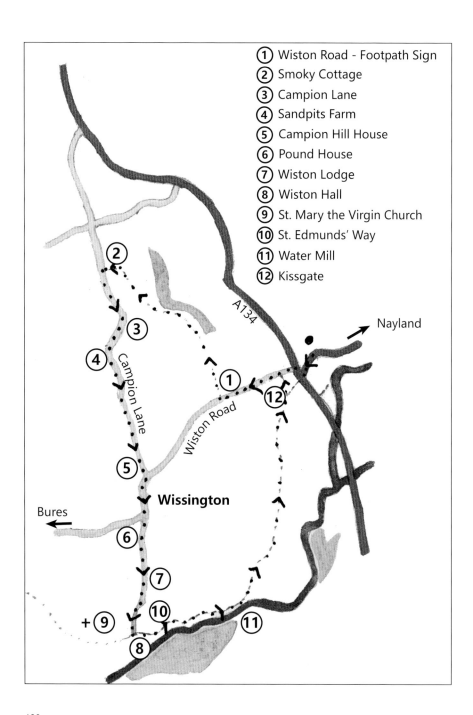

1. Wiston Road - Footpath Sign
2. Smoky Cottage
3. Campion Lane
4. Sandpits Farm
5. Campion Hill House
6. Pound House
7. Wiston Lodge
8. Wiston Hall
9. St. Mary the Virgin Church
10. St. Edmunds' Way
11. Water Mill
12. Kissgate

Nayland

A134

Campion Lane

Wiston Road

Wissington

Bures

hedge reveal grassy slopes where black rooks fly low. Across the valley a patchwork of biscuit brown fields are defined by hedges and rounded clumps of trees. A line of telegraph poles march into the distance.

5. Further down is Campion Hill House, where in her studio Rosie A. Childs creates fine artwork using photo collages, then comes Campion Farm – pale yellow behind a woven wicker fence ,where a holly tree grows. Here you join the Bures road. There is no pavement and is it quite busy so keep well in to the side.

6. Look out for a large black and white, thatched house. This was aptly called Corner House until renamed as Pound House. I wonder why? Here you cross the road and take the track beside it towards Wiston Church. To your right you will see the V.R. Post box where L. Harvey, among others, carved his name long ago.

There were fields of potatoes and patches of mayweed before a barns and another farmhouse appeared to the left. Four yellow arrows, in a vertical line on a pole directed me along a private, stony drive to Wiston Church. A sign invites you to park here for the church and a metal box awaits donated books. I peep inside, sadly it is empty.

7. You pass Wiston Lodge a pretty farm cottage with a stream running through its garden which was redirected when small children played there.

8. Ahead I can see a grand Georgian House, Wiston Hall.

9. I crunch on the gravel drive towards the Norman Church of St Mary the Virgin passing an old barn to the right. And what a wonderful country church this is! Surrounded by a profusion of

Wiston Lodge

unchecked wild flowers and ancient barns. Ronald Blythe, author of *Akenfield* said of it;

"This is as an old churchyard should be – so often they are too well kept."

Can you see a gravestone to Joshua George Harvey 1906-1989 (perhaps a link to the post box carver), beside Frank Woodgate a thatcher who entered eternal rest in 1983 aged 55. And another headstone carries the wonderful name of Olive, Gladys, Wilhelmina Blanche!

I entered the little church via a Norman wooden porch with a rounded archway. There were old photos here. I learned that The Rev. Charles Birch was responsible for the restoration that rounded the apse.

The Apse of the church

Inside are some thirteenth century wall paintings – and a 15th century dragon, who according to local legend killed sheep near to Bures in 1405 and a font with sleeping lions at its base. There is a Norman arch in the chancel but my attention was drawn to the inscribed slabs upon the floor.

Arthur Sadler of London. Gent. 1772.

Rev. William Barry. 1797. 60 years of his age.
Near 30 years vicar of this parish.
Peaceable disposition. Punctuality of duty.
By few equalled. Excelled by none!

Outside I found a wooden bench dedicated to Paul Rowland Taylor R.A F. whose fingers once played the organ here, but no more. He died many miles from this peaceful place in North Africa 1943.

Here I paused to sit in the warm sunshine and breathe in the tranquillity of my surroundings and I felt grateful for the life I enjoy. Before me were clouds of seeding grasses, purple knapweed and scabious and beyond them mossy, tiled sagging rooftops of low barns – a place to linger and simply BE.

10. Leave the churchyard and take the grassy stretch in front of red-bricked Wiston Hall. In 1786 it was given as a marriage gift to Samuel Beachcroft

by his father. Samuel went on to become the governor of the Bank of England in 1791.

This grassy path is called St Edmund's Way. It links to the Stour Valley Path. You will find a moat on your left and willows to your right.

11. You come to 18th century Wiston Water Mill hiding behind trees. It has a slate roof and weatherboarding. There was a mill first recorded here as early as 1352. It continued working until 1920. In the Middle Ages it was part of Wiston Manor. The mill stream still runs beneath it into the Mill pond. The house was once three cottages but in the 1920s was converted into one home.

Continue on, the river by your side. In autumn look for plump hazel nuts, clusters of small green berries on the buckthorn and purple sloes in the hedges. Cross a footbridge and walk through a plantation of young willows where the grass is shoulder-high and bees dance around tall teasels. On the bank of a stream in late summer months loosestrife flowers paint a splash of deep purple. The path creeps between overgrown brambles and tall thistles towards the sound of cars signalling the road ahead. Climb the stile into grazing land – a pasture to cross.

When I walked this way the black cows sat beneath the hedges motionless, bar their flicking ears as their heads slowly turning to follow my progress as swallows swooped low over the scrubby grass.

12. A kiss gate brings you back to the road and to the end of your walk.

WALK 18: HAWKEDON

Distance	3.5 miles or 5.6km
Time	Allow 2 hours at a gentle pace
Start	Outside The Queen's Head near the centre of the village
Terrain	Mainly up and down, steep in places
Map	OS Landranger 155
Refreshments	The Queen's Head serves food and drink
Toilets	No public loos – but the pub is handy!
Getting there	By car take the A1092 north of Cavendish or the A143 south of Chedburgh

Where the end of the Chiltern Hills rolls into East Anglia you'll find the beautiful landscape of High Suffolk and here is the pretty village of Hawkedon - a lovely walk in undulating farmland that crosses fields, treks along country lanes and both starts and ends in the village itself.

1. A good place to start is outside The Queen's Head (built around 1480). Here you can stop for some refreshment as you complete your walk. I leave my car there, by the roadside. (If you're there on a Friday or Saturday you could treat yourself to some good meat for the Old Post Office is now a butcher's shop.)

2. Opposite is Top Green Cottage, with a grey thatch and beside it The Old School House.

3. Walk down the road towards the church of St Mary's surrounded by its boundary wall and standing unusually, on the village green.

Top Green Cottage

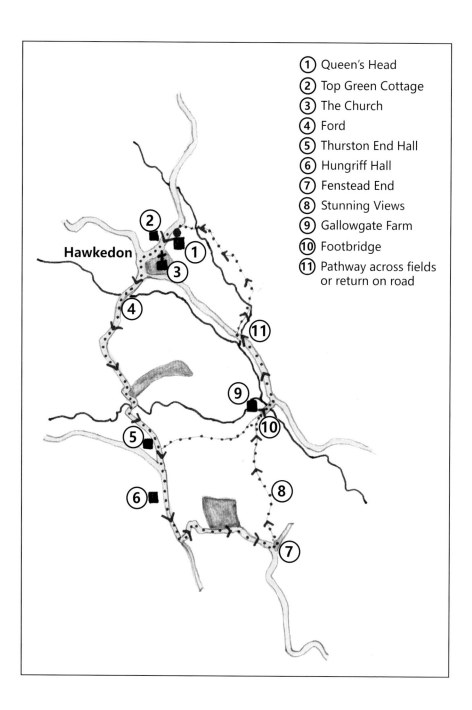

1. Queen's Head
2. Top Green Cottage
3. The Church
4. Ford
5. Thurston End Hall
6. Hungriff Hall
7. Fenstead End
8. Stunning Views
9. Gallowgate Farm
10. Footbridge
11. Pathway across fields or return on road

Hawkedon

I read that this church is one of Suffolk's best kept secrets – and when I stepped inside I was not disappointed. It is a simple Norman design, with a 14th century tower. There are no side aisles, no clerestory and the original font looks as if someone has chiselled off two of the square corners! But the fascinating features are the strange, elaborate carvings on the bench ends. A little man pokes out his tongue while two griffins salute him and there are two lions tied with thick rope as well as sad, noble faces and weird creatures clinging to the choir stalls. The east window contains some mediaeval glass and a wolf and eagle can be seen. The font is thought to be the original Norman font.

4. Outside follow the road around the green and down to a sign that says 'Deep Ford'. Here in the shadows of the trees is the river Glem. Then climb a steep rise up to wide, windswept, open farmland where, on a lovely autumn day, sunlight glows on the stubble and swallows swoop and skim and the only sound is the throb of a tiny faraway tractor. Purple knapweed and creamy-white bell-bine flowers tumble in the grassy verge.

5. Farther along this road, where aspen trees whisper in the wind, you will come to Thurston End Hall – a lovely old brick mansion – built in the 1500s

The church

on the site of a former hall, recorded in the Domesday Book – complete with a moat. The house we see today is Grade I Listed. It was altered in 1920 by Bernard Gaussen and his wife France-Doucha, a descendant of the Bonapartes. They added the scalloped barge boards to the gables. There are magnificent chimney stacks with ornamental herringbone red brick as well as diamond patterned, leaded light latticed windows. The three-storeyed porch was added in 1607. Inside is a Jacobean staircase and a huge inglenook fireplace.

6. There is a choice of route here. A bridleway to the left is a short cut across the field which brings you back to the walk. * If you stay on the road you will come to a junction. Turn left towards Glemsford. Look out for Hungriff Hall on your right. This is a symmetrical period farmhouse with gables. In December 1910, when it was occupied by a Mr Marsh, a fire in an over-heated chaff barn, brought Glemsford Fire Engine speeding to the rescue! The house was saved. In May 1911 the same Mr Marsh reported two labourers to the police. They had mischievously placed a heavy iron roller across the highway. PC Jolly found it and as it wasn't the first time such offences had been committed in Hawkedon the two men were fined forty shillings each!

I walked past a quaint thatched cottage where the smell of bacon wafted from an open latticed window. Hmm, breakfast seemed a long time ago – I suddenly felt hungry. The road curved past Hawkedon Plant Nursery (where you can buy beans, fresh eggs, cucumbers or local honey), then opened to another lovely vista of rolling farmland where the grey church tower rose above the trees. There were faraway white dots of cottages and a flash from a car windscreen, reflected the sun. A wood pigeon crooned in a nearby tree, its gentle sound adding to the sense of peace in this lovely place.

7. Soon you come to Fenstead End where you turn left onto a byway. Look for a footpath here which bears left between two barns. It follows a rough track by a stack of glistening straw bales and an old rusty roller, where seeding thistles grow amidst tall grasses.

8. *As the path plunged down into the valley, again the view before me was stunning; a patchwork of fields where cloud shadows drifted and tiny cattle grazed. In the blue sky scrawled wisps of fair-weather cirrus clouds and two buzzards circled in the thermals. The sun was hot on my back. I picked a ripe blackberry, its sweet-sharpness refreshing my mouth. A meadow brown butterfly fluttered about the pale purple flowers on the brambles.*

High Suffolk countryside

9. You will reach an iron gate. Watch where you place your feet, this is definitely cow pasture! Ahead is Gallowgate Farm with its rambling house and barns, and another gate. Here the short cut footpath joins our walk.* In the dark, gloomy shadows of the farm buildings are more bales and an old tractor. Walk through the farmyard quite close to the house and ahead you will see a footbridge and ford over the river.

Approach to Gallowgate Farm

10. *As I crossed the ford beside a makeshift footbridge (presumably there in case of flooding), the calves in the adjoining pasture galloped over to stare, curious at my passing. Their tails flicked away flies and their heads turned to follow my every step. As I came to the road again I caught the fragrance of honeysuckle tangled in the thick hedgerow.*

11. Turn left along the country road but look out for a footpath on the right.

(If you wish to avoid walking along the road side, which is the quicker and easier route, you can go this way across country.)

The track leads to a small gate and the path squeezes between a barbed wire fence and a deep ditch before it veers left across the field. Beware stinging nettles in summer. The path is not clearly marked here and it is hard to be sure of the correct route, but keep heading back towards the village on your far left. Walk around the field edge with a fence on your right until you see a footpath sign. Go into another field along a wide track with tall trees now to your left. This field you skirt to reach Hawkedon again. At the road turn left follow it up the slope back at the wisteria-clad Queen's Head where you began.

A few minutes later I was seated outside with a zingy lime and lemonade. Scott Chapman, the landlord for twelve years, told me that it was a coaching inn, on the road from Bury St. Edmunds to Long Melford. It is reputed that Queen Elizabeth I stayed here, hence the name.

The menu was chalked on a board. I note Muntjac and Guinness puff pot pie and strawberry and blueberry cheesecake. Scott said that pizzas were popular on Wednesday, Thursday and Sunday evenings but the weekend menu was more extensive; beef Wellington was the firm favourite. I also learned that the butcher's shop was part of the pub – Scott, a vegetarian said that he liked to use only well-reared local meat. Good for him!

I checked my watch. I still had time to buy some pork and sage sausages before the shop closed.

The three-and-a-half mile walk has taken two hours. I'm ready for grilled sausages and mushrooms with mashed potatoes and onion gravy – a fitting end to a lovely morning – where yet again Suffolk has surprised me with its unsung beauty.

WALK 19: EDWARDSTONE

Edweardstuna - the farmstead of Edward; another lovely circular walk on fields and in lanes - only a few miles from the beaten track - yet miles from anywhere!

1. A good place to start is the Millennium Green. There's a parking bay, an information board, children's playground, picnic tables, village sign, woodland walks; and there's the pub - just opposite!

Turn right and head towards The White Horse where daisies tumble untidily from a brick wall and a sticker in the door says 'Buy Local'. Behind the pub, in an old stable block is an enterprising little business - Mill Green

Distance	3.5 miles or 5.6km
Time	Allow 2 hours at an easy pace
Start	Millennium Green car park almost opposite The White Horse
Terrain	Fairly level, with gentle slopes
Map	OS Landranger 155
Refreshments	The White Horse. Open all day
Toilets	The pub
Getting there	By car. Take the A1071 from Sudbury to Hadleigh. Look for the signpost and take the road through Boxford

Eco-Brewery. I read that it has been given several awards including SIBA's best mild ale in East Anglia.

I did this walk on a beautiful, blue-sky morning in spring. The sun was warm. The blackthorn hedgerows were adorned with smoky clouds of white blossom. The air vibrated with birdsong and somewhere a wood pigeon crooned; 'I love you, darling.'

The White Horse

Go pass a pond on your right, then head out of the village to open farmland and gentle Suffolk fields.

Soon you see Hilly Farm on the right but go straight on along the twisting country road edged with neatly trimmed hedges and banks of primroses.

2. You come to The Flushing Farm, where horse chestnut trees have leaf buds curled tight like clenched fists, then at Round Maple, a junction. Turn left by a 17th century pink thatched cottage called Seasons. An open gate beneath an archway leads into the unseen garden.

The road meanders between fields and a verge of wild flowers; stitchwort (shirt-buttons); bluebells, yellow cowslips (pagles) and the poisonous dark green leaves of dog's mercury.

3. Beyond a stream the road ascends to Quick's Farm with its neatly mowed paddock behind white railings where the last daffodils were in bloom.

4. You reach Grove Cottage, another manicured garden, its entrance marked by a trailing willow tree of spring green. If you'd like to linger longer there are self-catering holiday-lets here.

Now it's time to leave the road and trek across a field towards the church. The farmer had left a path between his crops.

It was muddy here and the lumps of heavy clay stuck to my boots – I wondered if perhaps I should have stayed on the road which I presently re-joined? I scraped off some mud before turning left.

5. At a fork in the road, where some pretty red-bricked cottages stand on the corner behind their little white gates, bear right and you come to The Old School House.

Here my curiosity got the better of me. I spied a gentleman in the garden and wandered up the drive. I asked him about the house. He told me that the school closed in 1958.

"Did you know my wife is a potter?" he continued, "come and meet her".

Although unannounced, Sandy Larkman greeted me with a beaming smile and led me into the house. She showed me the old classrooms with their original floors; then we went into her studio to see her vibrant paintings of flowers. On the easel was a half completed study of purple anemones. Sandy gave me a peep into the pottery studio where she runs courses. People who are battling with the effect of a stroke come to Sandy for pottery classes.

"I have probably learned as much from these wonderful people as they have from me", she said.

Sandy told me that they bought the house from the artist Edward Middleditch.

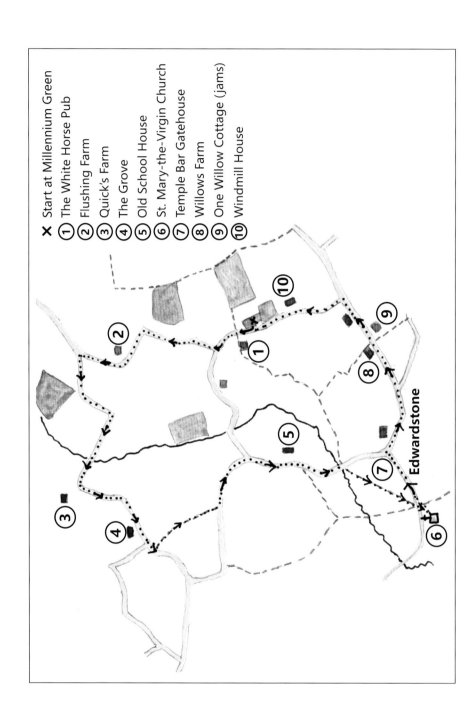

X Start at Millennium Green
① The White Horse Pub
② Flushing Farm
③ Quick's Farm
④ The Grove
⑤ Old School House
⑥ St. Mary-the-Virgin Church
⑦ Temple Bar Gatehouse
⑧ Willows Farm
⑨ One Willow Cottage (jams)
⑩ Windmill House

Edwardstone

"He was Keeper of the Royal Academy School of Art. It is an honour to work in his studio", she adds. Sandy's work can be seen at the Suffolk Show and in local exhibitions. She also takes private commissions.

I thank them both for their kind welcome then continue my stroll taking the second footpath on the right, beside a gurgling brook where marsh marigolds show golden flowers. The sign on the stile says; Bull in field. Enter at your own risk. I spy him and he isn't far away but he is surrounded by cows and calves. The grassy meadow leads up to the church and I have planned to visit it so I quicken my pace, keeping a wary eye on the heavy-shouldered fellow who disdainfully ignores me!

6. Once over the stile the path tracks diagonally across the damp grass until you reach an old iron kiss gate. Follow the lane to St Mary the Virgin Church (recorded in Domesday) but do stop, look back to enjoy the far-reaching views over undulating Suffolk countryside. A beautiful scene.

The church was first built by Anglo-Saxons, then rebuilt in the 14th century, using some recycled roman bricks before being rebuilt again around 1870.

The path to the church

Inside is a 13th century font with a Jacobean cover.

I climbed into the carved pulpit then found a little book for prayer requests – each one with a thoughtful response written by an unknown hand. I added my own request.

The Temple Bar Gatehouse and me!

7. Outside follow the gravel drive, edged by iron railings to the Temple Bar Gatehouse with its arched entrance, ornate windows; octagonal tower and Victorian post box. It once marked the entrance to the original Edwardstone Hall, demolished in 1952. Here you bear right and follow the road until you reach another junction and the war memorial. Keep straight on for the village. Again you can see for miles and miles wherever you look.

8. On your left you will see Willows Farm, then across the road, in the porch
& of One Willow Cottage homemade preserves in attractively labelled jars
9. are for sale.

There was apricot chutney, damson jam and lemon and lime marmalade. I perused the choice and settled for the marmalade.

Now you are back in the village with some lovely thatched little cottages with clues to their past in their names; Jimmy's, Old Forge Cottage, Moot Cottage and Moat Farm Cottage. Look out for a road sign, Mill Green View.

I am assuming there must be a mill of some description somewhere! Meanwhile gardens full of tulips and bluebells, magnolias and forsythia add to the beauty. From the back of an open van at Tudor Cottage came radio music – a gentle guitar and a voice singing 'The Sound of Silence'. A man in white-splashed overalls carried a large tin of paint towards the house. Someone's busy!

10. Take the next left turn and soon you'll see Mill Green Cottage (there is it again) where blue grape hyacinths edge the borders. Then you come to it, the answer to the mystery – Windmill House! A sensible-looking red-brick family home on the right. Mystery solved!

One of the pretty cottages

I took a deep breath and marched up the drive. It was a day for boldness! A young man answered the door. I introduced myself then fired my question.

"Please can you tell me about the windmill?"

Justin was happy to talk then disappeared inside to find an old photograph he had recently acquired. The mill was demolished in 1965. We stood outside on the spot where the photo was taken. I thanked him and continued my walk.

A few more steps along the road will take you back to the starting place, the Millennium Green.

I ended my walk at The White Horse by sitting outside at a wooden picnic bench, sipping a cold shandy and soaking up the hot sun.

WALK 20: CAVENDISH

This circular walk begins and ends in one of the prettiest, picture postcard villages in Suffolk – Cavendish. It explores beautiful undulating countryside with amazing views of farmland. It follows country lanes (no pavement) and crosses fields.

1. Leave the main road in the centre of the village, by the green and the pretty pink alms houses to park beneath the leafy trees near the church of St Mary the Virgin. It was built in the Perpendicular style around the 15th century on the site of a Saxon Church dated about 1086. There are Roman bricks in its walls and both the tower and south porch are 14th century. Inside is a plaque unveiled in honour of Sue Ryder and her husband

Distance	3.5 miles or 5.6 km.
Time	Allow 2 hours at a gentle pace
Start	Park near the church or village green
Terrain	An up and down walk with some level stretches
Map	OS Landranger 155
Refreshments	Local pubs; The Bull, The Five Bells and The George
Toilets	No public toilets
Getting there	The 236 bus runs from Haverhill to Sudbury and the 374 from Bury St Edmunds to Clare. By car drive along the A1092 – between Clare and Long Melford

Leonard Cheshire who are buried here. They lived in Devonshire House in the main street.

2. Head up the slight gradient of Peacock's Road which leads out of the village towards a pink timbered house (1350) called Nether Hall once the home of George Cavendish. It is one of those perfect days in late spring,

Cottages and church

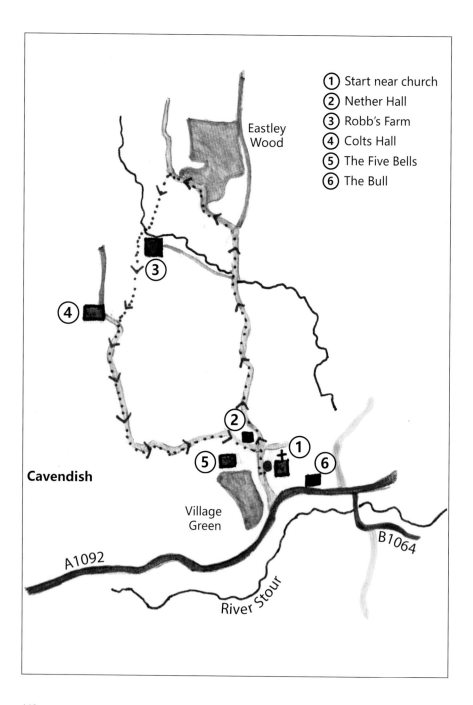

① Start near church
② Nether Hall
③ Robb's Farm
④ Colts Hall
⑤ The Five Bells
⑥ The Bull

Eastley Wood

Cavendish

Village Green

A1092

River Stour

B1064

with blue sky and high wisps of feathery clouds. Sparrows chirrup noisily in the hedges and delicate, white stitchwort grows among the profusion of wild flowers that edge the pathway. Soon open fields appear.

The final house is clearly the home of an impressive gardener! I marvel at the vegetables standing to attention in neat rows and the FOUR wheelbarrows!

The narrow road climbs between banks of dandelions, white dead nettles and the lace of cow parsley where a fat bumble bee grumbles his way. Pause to look back and see the village rooftops below and views of gentle farmland open far and wide on either side.

As I do this a skylark suddenly sings as if exalting in the space and beauty that surrounds us both.

To my left nestled down in the valley, the buildings of Robb's Farm comes into view.

This is why I have come to Cavendish. I recently had a conversation with a neighbour of mine; an elderly man called Tom Doe. As he recounted his long-ago memories, he mentioned Robb's Farm. It was once his home.

He *chuckled as he recalled his time there. "The farm came up for sale during the Second World War. My father bought it and moved in with mother and us four children – though there was no water or electricity. Somehow we managed. He built a tower to house a water tank – which is still there I believe. We even kept a house cow."*

During one year Tom remembers three aeroplanes crashing in the fields around their home. In March 1944 an old Short Stirling took off from nearby RAF Stradishall with a crew of seven men. In a heavy snowstorm, ice caused an engine to fail and they had to bale out.

"There were belts of ammunition draped all over the trees and the stink of petrol running down the road", Tom told me – a faraway look in his watery eyes.

A few weeks later a German JU88 A-4 Werke flying low on a bombing mission, was shot down. The fuel tank exploded and both the pilot and radio

Robb's Farm

operator were killed but two airmen FW Maser and FW Elmshorst baled out and survived to be captured by the Home Guard, which included Tom and his father.

In July of the same year a B24 Bomber, based at an airfield in Lavenham collided with a Flying Fortress during a practice flight. It too crashed here and the crew were killed. The next day Tom found an expensive brown leather shoe, at the far side of the field. He took it home. A few hours later he found the second shoe close to the mangled metal of the wreckage.

"Would you believe it? They fitted me perfectly. I had them a long time! Dead Man's Shoes!" He chuckled again.

One barn was given over to house Italian prisoners of war and Tom remembers playing lively games of football with them. His mother used to cook huge bowls of spaghetti to make them feel at home.

Another barn served as a school. Although Tom was too old, his younger brother, Will attended it.

You will see the driveway that leads to the little farm with its outbuildings, water tower and barns, but keep tramping up the country road for the map shows two footpaths further on, the second one doubles back and passes close behind Robb's farm itself.

The road bears left and Eastley Wood appears on your right, in spring full of beautiful bluebells and bird song. Ignore the first footpath across the field on your left and take the bridleway sign that points towards Robb's Farm.

I found the path was not well trodden but it took me to the far edge where a wooden bridge crosses a stream. A glance at my watch tells me I have been walking for nearly an hour.

3. Now I can see the farm. The barns have been converted into smart, weather-boarded homes but the farm house itself has probably changed little since Tom's day. It retains an old-fashioned charm about it. The path continues steeply up a huge field of young wheat. Stop to catch your breath and look back to see faraway farms and distant grey woodlands rolling away, away up to the sky.

4. You will reach a hedgerow entwined with thorny brambles and walk towards Colt's Hall. In the 13th century this was part of a big estate owned

Wide open farmland

by William de Grey, a knight. The path way here becomes very overgrown and the house is well screened by trees.

A yellow Brimstone butterfly flutters across my way. I can hear moorhens so there must be water nearby. Yes, here is the pond edged with tangled undergrowth and tall rushes.

Press on to find an old wooden signpost that offers a confusing choice of direction. Turn right onto a small tarmacked lane that drops down to the village below. From this high spot the views across the Stour valley are stunning. There is a neatly clipped hedge on your right.

As I pass a wheat field I hear a rustling noise and see the tall green spears stirring. Something unseen is moving. I stand still. Then I see them; four hares racing about like mad things. One veers away and charges straight towards me - completely unaware of my presence. I hold my breath. It jumps the ditch and almost lands at my feet before it sees me. Glints of gold flash in its eye as startled, it dashes away in alarm. A moment to remember.

The road begins to climb again and the sun is warm - in a baby-blue sky.

I wonder if Group Captain Leonard walked here in this peaceful place, a far cry from the battlefield and the years of The Second World War? He flew 102 missions and became known for his 'supreme contempt of danger'. He commanded the 617 dam-busters Squadron, but resigned from the RAF as a protest after the Nagasaki nuclear attack. He achieved the highest award for gallantry; the Victoria Cross and later became Baron Cheshire because of his charity work.

Sue Ryder, the young woman who lied about her age of fifteen because she wanted to volunteer her services to the First Aid Nursing Yeomanry, found herself in Poland, tending wounded soldiers. She joined the Special Operations Executive and her job was to drive agents to airfields.

In 1953 she established the Sue Ryder Foundation and today there about eight thousand volunteers, eighty homes and five hundred Sue Ryder charity shops, including one here in Cavendish in the old cinema building. In this idyllic place she opened a home here for concentration camp survivors which later became a nursing home. She too was honoured as a life peer in 1979 and awarded the OBE.

At Mumford Cottages, where washing blows on the line, the chimneys of Cavendish can be clearly seen. Now you pass the back gardens of houses behind a steep bank on your left. *The church clock strikes twelve above the sound of passing traffic. I've been walking about two hours. To my right is the familiar sight of the ancient Nether Hall and just around the corner is the churchyard and my little car.*

5. You could enjoy a drink outside The Five Bells with its picnic tables overlooking the sloping grass of the village green but 'The Bull' (6) – an old-fashioned red brick pub, serves a two-course meal at lunch time or simply tea and coffee.

Today's menu of Mediterranean quiche with buttered new potatoes and salad, sounds tempting, as does orange and chocolate cheesecake. I think I may delay my homeward journey ... but if I wanted to make a weekend of it; The George provides dinner, bed and breakfast deals during October to March. Now there's a thought.

Tom Doe died at the age of eighty-nine in May 2016.

Nether Hall

WALK 21: GROTON

Today I am in Groton or Grotenea (sandy stream in Anglo Saxon). This ancient settlement, a cluster of small hamlets, is brimming with clues to its past. I aim to discover some of Groton's hidden secrets.

A circular walk along country lanes, field edges, in woodland and across meadows.

1. Take the road north from Boxford and on a sharp right hand bend is The Fox and Hounds. It has a car park and a friendly landlord. Check with him that you can leave your car before taking the narrow road to Groton beside

Distance	3.6 miles or 5.8km
Time	1½ to 2 hours, depending on pace
Start	Car park of Fox and Hounds
Terrain	Gentle ups and downs
Map	OS Landranger 155
Refreshments	Fox and Hounds
Toilets	No public toilets
Getting there	By car. Turn off A1071 at Boxford. Follow the road to Groton bearing left in centre of Boxford. Drive up a hill about half a mile to find the Fox and Hounds

the pub. Walk past several cottages and the back gateway to the 15th century church of St Bartholomew.

Soon you will see a footpath sign pointing right, this is where you leave the road and enter Groton Croft, owned by the Groton Winthrop Mulberry Trust.

Fox and Hounds

A muddy path, edged with luxuriant cow parsley leads into a grassy meadow, where an abundance of wild flowers bloom.

The croft seeks to provide; 'a place of quiet enjoyment in perpetuity'. But its centre piece is the mulberry tree surrounded by a fence. A plaque informs me that it came from Persia and was planted during the reign of Elizabeth I by Adam Winthrop. The old tree has twisted branches now daubed with yellow and grey lichen but there are signs of life for buds are forming and I am told it still bears fruit. I learn that the Mulberry tree is a food source for silk worms.

Follow the trodden path near to the spot where a Gloster Meteor F8 fighter jet crashed in May 1953. There are notice boards dotted around to tell you

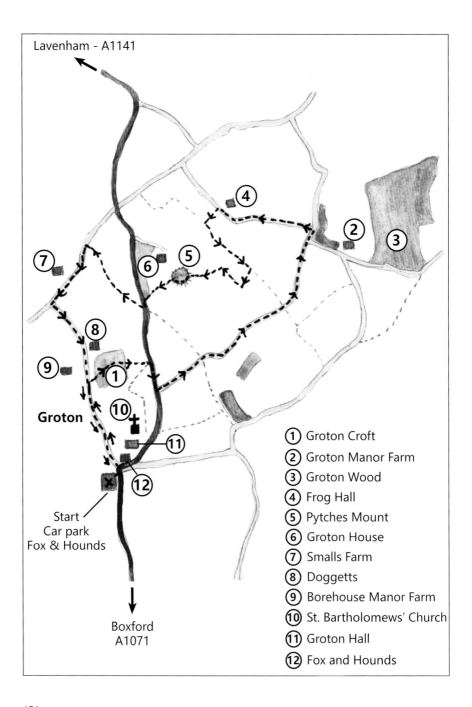

Lavenham - A1141

⑦ Smalls Farm
⑥ Groton House
⑤ Pytches Mount
④ Frog Hall
② Groton Manor Farm
③ Groton Wood
⑧ Doggetts
⑨ Borehouse Manor Farm
① Groton Croft
Groton
⑩ St. Bartholomews' Church
⑪ Groton Hall
⑫ Fox and Hounds

X Start
Car park
Fox & Hounds

Boxford
A1071

① Groton Croft
② Groton Manor Farm
③ Groton Wood
④ Frog Hall
⑤ Pytches Mount
⑥ Groton House
⑦ Smalls Farm
⑧ Doggetts
⑨ Borehouse Manor Farm
⑩ St. Bartholomews' Church
⑪ Groton Hall
⑫ Fox and Hounds

of the history of this place. I read that the pilot, George Pullen ejected and survived. Walk across the grassy space.

At a gate turn right onto the road. After a few steps take a left turn towards Castlings Heath and amble along between wide open fields as the road rolls down to a stream then climbs again. You will

Walking in open countryside

see a house called The Spong. Look back to enjoy panoramic views across the undulating countryside to the church and rooftops of Groton.

Soon you will come to a barn where brambles arch and cling to the wall. Follow the roller-coaster road towards Dove Barn.

When I walked here early oil seed rape flowers painted yellow streaks across the distant green fields and in the verge Lords and Ladies poked skywards through the new grass and dog's mercury. Down in the valley to my right sparkles of sunlight glinted on the little brook. A chaffinch sang from a high bough in a willow tree bearing soft flowering plumes.

2. Look out for Groton Manor Farm hiding in trees and beyond it. Groton
& Wood is managed by Suffolk Wildlife Trust. (This is another walk, for
3. another day. It is a fine example of a Medieval woodland with small-leaved lime trees, indeed a secret place of orchids and dormice.)

4. At a junction turn left, then left again to follow a by-road past Castlings Heath Cottage. In spring bluebells flower along the hedgerow. The road dips down to a copse where there is a pretty thatched cottage – a scene lifted straight from a children's fairy story book. It is called Frog Hall and bears a date 1650. Perhaps a frog prince once dwelt within?

Leave the lane to follow a muddy footpath on the left, imprinted with many horses' hooves. A wooden bridge of planks takes you along the lower edge of a field of seeding grasses. Follow the hedge line until you come to another wooden plank bridge. Turning right, cross the stream to tramp up the green slope towards the woodland that hides Pytches Mount. Follow little arrow signs passing jumps for horses, to follow the field edge then head towards the overgrown woodland from whence the unmistakeable call of a chiff-chaff drifts.

5. Half hidden by trees and undergrowth is the mound of a Norman motte and bailey castle that stood here in the 12th century. The path becomes somewhat obscure here but search for a gap in the hedge and an access point enabling you to scramble up the twenty foot high concave earthworks and enjoy the commanding views of the countryside all around.

I had spotted Pytches Mount on my map but it was much bigger than I expected, some 200 feet in diameter. There are no information boards but I have read that the Pecche family owned it in the 12th century. Although it is a scheduled ancient monument it has become just one of those forgotten places that seemed to whisper secrets from long ago. On the top I stood quietly and imagined days when watchmen looked out over the far-reaching landscape. I wondered what adventures happened here in the faraway past? Now it is the home for rabbits, badgers and more brambles.

6. Back on ground level circle the motte until you find a stile. Keeping Groton House to your right wander through a spinney where a stile takes you

St Bartholomew's Church

across rough pasture to reach an old wooden gate and another muddy path, which leads to a road. Here cross over to a footpath sign pointing right. Walk along a deep ditch line where primroses cascade down the steep bank. A blackbird sings in a clump of tall poplar trees.

Soon you reach another narrow lane. Turn left. (A red-bricked bungalow is nearby.)

7. A short walk brings you to Smalls Farm where, in springtime, lilies float on the pond. If you look across the landscape here you can retrace your route. A little further on look for a turning towards Boxford which will take you back to the houses of Groton.

8. One impressive building is Doggetts, the ancestral home of Richard Doggett. Its Georgian façade hides a 1450 interior. In 1540 the two separate wings were linked by the central hall to give us the grand house we see today. It was sold to John Winthrop, grandson of Adam Winthrop (a wealthy clothier in Lavenham, who was made Lord of Groton Manor in 1544 by Henry VIII).

It is thought that John, who was the first Justice of the Peace, lived in Doggetts until he led the Puritan emigration to New England in 1630. Although Elizabeth I had reinstated Protestantism the cobwebs of ecclesiastical liturgy still lingered in the churches and provoked the mass migration of people seeking a simpler style of worship. John Winthrop founded Boston and became the first governor of the Massachusetts Bay Colony.

A novel by Anya Seaton called 'The Winthrop Woman' tells a remarkable story, if you are interested to know more.

9. Look out for Borehouse Manor Farm on your left before you come to the gate to Groton Croft, where this circular walk really began.

When I walked sheep grazed as their new-born lambs raced about like mad things in little gangs.

10. The Fox and Hounds is not far away but you may wish to visit the 15th century St Bartholomew's church, a little further along the road. Here you will find memorials to the Winthrop family including heraldry and a

Victorian stained glass window to the memory of John Winthrop, born in Groton Manor in 1587. The disillusioned Puritans fled from England during the reign of Charles 1. The link to Boston, Massachusetts is still very much alive today indeed there is a town called Groton in the USA when settlers claimed the land there in 1655. It was then called The Plantation of Groton. People come from there to visit this little village. The church has been funded by the Winthrop family to this day, and is in excellent repair. There is no original glass but do look for the American Indian chief carved into the ironwork!

11. Beside the church is Groton Hall, a fine old farmhouse with an assortment
& of outbuildings where white doves fly. A few steps takes you back to the
12. Fox and Hounds and your car. Do stop to gaze over the valley and linger with some refreshment!

Walk 22: Poslingford

On the road towards Bury St Edmunds and just beyond the last houses of Clare you'll find a narrow lane that climbs for a mile before you reach Poslingford – another of Suffolk's secrets. I went one cold day when winter was tentatively thinking about becoming spring. I left my car in The Street, outside the Old School House, right opposite St Mary's Church where early daffodil spears showed amidst pale primroses.

Once upon a time this village had a school, a Post Office, a shop and a blacksmiths as well as the pub. A far cry from the Poslingford we visit today.

A circular route that could be describes as an 'upper and downer'. It is mainly on tiny country lanes but also crosses (sometimes muddy) fields.

Distance	4 miles or 6.4km
Time	2 hours
Start	In the main street park by roadside near the church
Terrain	Very up and down
Map	OS Landranger 155
Refreshments	Nearby Clare has tea shops and pubs
Toilets	No public toilets
Getting there	By car. A1092 to Clare then B1063 to Bury St Edmunds

1. Park your car in the middle of the village where a little stream runs alongside the road. Look for the Old School (complete with bell) where there were two classes when The Second World War began. Mrs Dunn taught the old'ns and Miss Rodgers the little 'uns, and postman Bert Martin cycled up the hill from Clare twice every day to deliver the mail. During the war itself evacuees stayed in the school house. When the children reached the age of eleven they had to walk the two miles to Clare school every day, come rain or shine.

Set off up the hill towards Stansfield and you will pass by a few houses and the former pub, The Shepherd and His Dog, now a pink- painted home. Look out for some pretty thatched cottages behind old, rambling apple trees where noisy sparrows chirp. This walk will take you to Chipley Abbey then swerves across wide open countryside to bring you back to the shelter of the village. There is a steep bank edging the road which is steadily climbing higher and soon the views open on either side.

A wide sweep of spring-green fields rose and fell with the contours of the land. A line of tiny telegraph poles marched across the far reaching field, adding to the sense of distance. As I reached a gap in the hedge the cold wind (which was roaring in the tree tops) hit me with a mighty gust as I felt its full force! Head down, I battled on!

At a junction turn left to Assington Green. Thankfully the road drops and soon it becomes more sheltered. To your left is the church tower already far away. There are very sharp bends as the narrow lane follows the boundaries of the empty ploughed fields. Small streams trickle on either side.

2. You will come to a fork and the walk continues to the right but pause here to take a diversion to see Chipley Abbey Farm built on the site of a small Augustine Priory founded in 1235. By 1455 the priory had been abandoned and the buildings were in ruins. The chapel was used (somewhat irreverently) to house the cows until it was demolished in 1818. Today nothing remains but the 17th century farmhouse, built with ancient, recycled material and part of a west wall that once stood in the monastery, but within St Mary's church in the village is a stone coffin and bell that once tolled here.

3. Look out for a memorial stone among the laurel bushes and Scots Pines that line the drive. It was erected to remember the Clopton family. The

The Main Street

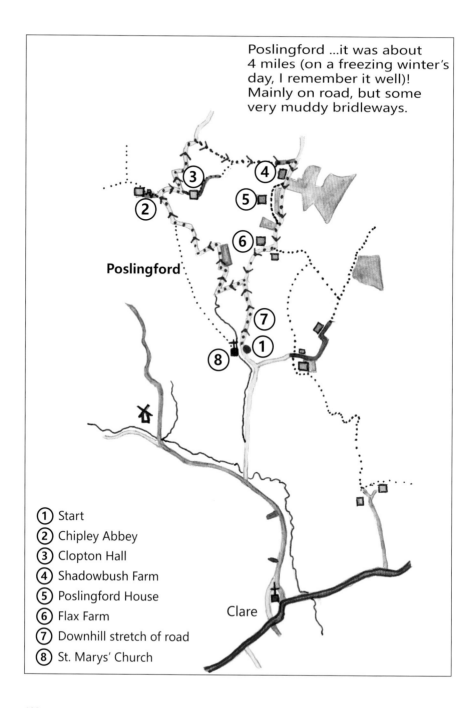

Poslingford ...it was about 4 miles (on a freezing winter's day, I remember it well)! Mainly on road, but some very muddy bridleways.

Poslingford

Clare

(1) Start
(2) Chipley Abbey
(3) Clopton Hall
(4) Shadowbush Farm
(5) Poslingford House
(6) Flax Farm
(7) Downhill stretch of road
(8) St. Marys' Church

inscription tells passing walkers that many of the Cloptons are buried here, the Sir Williams and Sir Walters of the 1300s together with their wives.

4. Retrace your steps to the lane that passes farm cottages (1880). Round a bend you will see Clopton Hall with a thick box hedge arching the front door. Behind the façade is a 17th timber framed house. A former hall, Cloptuna was recorded in the Domesday Book in 1086 when there were 54 houses in Poslingford.

Just beyond the house, suddenly I saw them – thick clumps of delicate snowdrops in the verge and on the roof of a tumbledown log cabin and in white drifts beneath the apples trees in the garden. Sheer beauty! Such a reward for winter walkers!

Arched gateway

The road leads to Gosland Green and you'll come to a footpath going left beside a hedge which serves as a boundary for a garden. Time to leave the road and follow the field edge until the path heads straight across the field itself. Head for the far gap!

My footprints joined many others, deer and fox and perhaps badger. Little yellow signs assured me I was on route. Because of the rain on the previous day my boots became heavier with each step, this was real clay mud – the kind that sticks in slippery lumps. But away across the fields was a faraway view of the valley if I lifted my eyes for a moment, as I picked my way carefully around deep puddles.

5. Soon you will see farm buildings ahead and then thankfully an end to the mud as the road appears. This is Shadowbush Farm. Here you turn right.

6. Behind a fenced woodland screen you can get a glimpse of Poslingford
& House. During The Second World War a Mustang hit a tree here and
7. crashed into a field – killing the pilot, Flying Officer Weston.

You soon come to a cottage with a mossy thatched roof. Beneath a low window stands a rustic bench.

Look out for Flax Farmhouse. Here you can just see the church and rooftops of Poslingford – they seem a very long way off and in the far distance is Clare but be encouraged, you are on the home stretch now and the road gently takes you down to the village.

8. Before you leave Poslingford, visit St Mary's Church with its attractive 15th century red brick porch, flint tower and 12th century lancet window. Inside is a 12th century font and the stone coffin already mentioned as well as the tomb of Mary Golding who married a cavalier, Sir George Villiers. Hopefully the door will be unlocked.

In 2014 some archaeologists carried out an excavation some sixty metres from the church. Among the treasure was 12/13th century pottery, medieval post holes and a golden ring.

As there was no place to rest or find refreshment in Poslingford I drove back to Clare where I was soon enjoying a welcome hot chocolate topped with a generous helping of cream and marshmallows in The Antiques Centre tea

Thatched cottage

room tucked away down Maltings Lane (not far from Clare Castle Country Park). Here there are the remains of a 13th century stone castle on a high motte.

I treated myself to a scone, thick with yellow butter and dollops of strawberry jam. After all, I reckoned I'd walked about four miles on a cold winter's day! I warmed up as I mooched around the antique stands where assorted Royal Doulton Toby jugs grinned at me. In a glass cabinet old rings sparkled; Burmese rubies and chocolate quartz and suspended from nails in the ceiling were wooden chairs, bellows and a birdcage. You could even buy an antique hippo tooth! (what would I do with that?)

I strolled along the High Street pausing to window shop. There are several interesting little shops in Clare selling homeware and pretty cards.

I returned to my car and parked by J.R. Humphreys and Sons, the butchers where you can buy squirrel, partridges and pheasants as well as 'Moo and Blue Pies' (beef and Stilton). Squirrel ... hmm! Another day perhaps!

WALK 23: HARTEST

Hartest (Stag's Wood) is an ancient settlement. The first recorded church stood there in 1086. It is in High Suffolk, one of the prettiest corners of this lovely county. There are about fifty listed buildings here. Three of the farms can be traced back to 1320s. In the 1841 census there were twenty-four farms in Hartest and indeed this remains an agricultural area today.

The Crown was once the Moot Hall and Manor House. There are old photos telling you about its past, within. In 1597 a John Bridge left it to his son, William.

The All Saints Church, not far from the green, that you see today in mainly 15th century. There is Tudor brick work repairing older walls. It has an actagonal two tier Jacobean pulpit. It is worth a visit. To the south of the church is the rectory and beyond the river, the steepest hill in Suffolk! If you bother to climb it you will be rewarded with stunning views.

This is a more strenuous walk up hill and down dale, around fields and along country lanes in stunning scenery that both starts and finished in the lovely village.

Distance	4 miles or 6.4km
Time	2 hours +
Start	Village green in centre of Hartest
Terrain	Ups and downs all the way – rarely flat – but never really steep
Map	OS Explorer 211
Refreshments	The Crown public house
Toilets	No public toilets
Getting there	374 bus from Clare or Bury St Edmunds. Or by car via the B1066

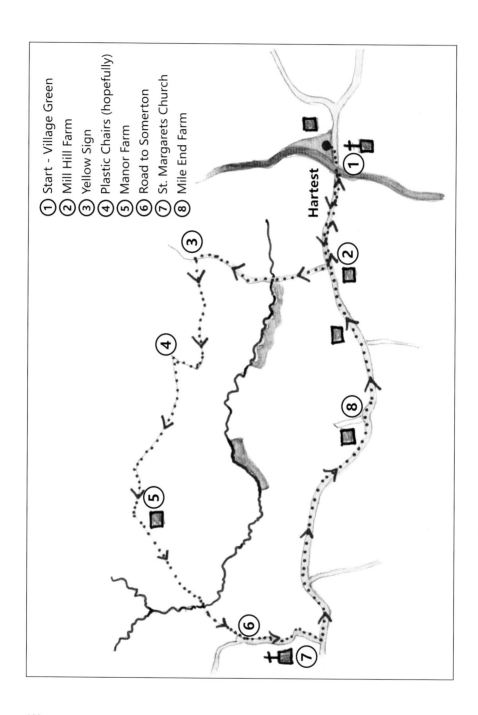

1 Start - Village Green
2 Mill Hill Farm
3 Yellow Sign
4 Plastic Chairs (hopefully)
5 Manor Farm
6 Road to Somerton
7 St. Margarets Church
8 Mile End Farm

Hartest

1. Leave the car by the green central to the village, edged with lovely picture postcard properties and take the narrow road to Somerton, the neighbouring village which has a long standing link with Hartest. You will pass the Institute on your right. Look out for the village sign to your left. This road leads up and away from the cluster of houses. Within minutes, a far-reaching panorama of Suffolk farmland can seen on either side beyond stubble fields. You will soon see a red pan-tiled roof ahead.

2. This denotes Mill Hill Farmhouse and here you turn right off the road to walk down a wide track which is a public footpath. This is Smith-brook Lane. It dips down between fields to a stream.

3. Keep straight up the slope, where nettles line the pathway, until you see a brick wall in front of you. Here (at a yellow restricted by-way sign), turn left and tramp along a wide grassy verge beside the field. Look down across the valley to see Mill Hill Farm.

When I walked this way, in the vast sky a buzzard circled, wings outstretched, 'mewing' his call. Wild flowers added to the beauty; rusty-brown ribwort plantains with delicate collars of white anthers; sulphur-

Cottages edge the Green

yellow daisy heads of common ragwort and pinky-purple knapweed all jostling for position along the field edge.

The path drops to the valley and leads into another field.

4. I smell newly-ploughed earth. Then I am climbing again towards two white plastic chairs, up-ended at the hedge-line. *How kind! Just what I needed – somewhere to take a breather. I sit and gaze at the lovely countryside falling and rising up to the blue sky adorned with towering white clouds. Across the broad sweeps of farm land with isolated farmsteads comes the sound of a faraway tractor. Apart from that – stillness. This is truly a beautiful place to simply be.*

   Continue into the next field where an oak stands marooned to the right. This is a rare place – there are no signs of human habitation; no pylons, rooftops, not even a church spire. Suffolk at its finest as it was before people built their homesteads.

5. Soon you will see a house ahead and a gap on its right. Here you edge round a pond and come to Manor Farm. A yellow sign points left. Walk by a tumble down barn and a house. Look out for another footpath sign to confirm you are on track.

   Lining the footpath there are trumpets of white bindweed flowers twisting around white daisies and clumps of common toadflax (a bit like yellow snap-dragons) where a brown gatekeeper butterfly flits. Beyond a telegraph pole is a cottage with a line of white washing, billowing in the wind.

6. Cross the stream and reach a quiet road where you turn left (towards Clare) and climb towards Somerton. It is a little steep here.

   Gravel crunches beneath my boots. It's taken about an hour so far. Here is a small hamlet of cottages and I smile at an amusing sign – in French, on a wooden gate on my right.

7. Soon the St Margaret's church will appear. It is mainly early English but with a blocked Norman door in the nave and shafts of 13th century windows in the east wall. It also has an unusual double chancel. Do take time to wander into the churchyard, overgrown with seeded grasses. Ivy cleaves to old leaning headstones. There are sturdy brick buttresses

daubed with golden sunburst lichen. The nearby war memorial reminds us of three local lads killed within a space of three months, one from Mile End Farm. Another, Jesse Stiff, who died in Palestine in December 1917 aged twenty-nine.

As I enter the porch a pigeon explodes from a nest above me. I'm not sure who is most surprised! The door is locked.

Back on the road bear right and look out for the pump and some newer houses to your left.

The village sign gives me another smile! Can you spot the mistake?

Now you are walking back to Hartest, along a delightful open road. Here you can enjoy High Suffolk and see why it is so named. Across the valley to your left you can trace the route you have taken, including the dots of white chairs (If they are still there)!

8. You will reach Mile End Farmhouse. A massive granite boulder was dug up here in High Field and this stone became the link between the two villages! In 1713 it was dragged on a purpose-built sledge by forty or more horses down the hill to Hartest green with a Mr. Marks of Rivets Hall seated upon it – blowing a trumpet to celebrate the victories of the Duke of Marlborough that ended of the long war of the Spanish Succession. This was when Great

The road back to Hartest

Britain claimed Gibraltar. The whole village celebrated for the rest of the day and longer! There were joyous celebrations throughout the whole land. The huge stone is still there, on the green outside a pretty cottage - see photo on page 169. (There is a long-standing record of 21 people standing on it at once)!

You will pass Charity Farmhouse before you come back to Mill Hill Farm and Smith-brook Lane where the across country route began. Keep on this road sloping gently down into Hartest.

9. *I'd walked some four miles in about two hours. A thatched cottage (1795) signals the village and delicious smells came from The Crown where soon I was enjoying Cider and Cauliflower Soup with thickly buttered, fresh granary bread. It became a pub in the 18th century, prior to that it was the Manor House. There is a big garden with picnic tables and play equipment – perfect for families on sunny days.*

The Crown

10. *Refreshed, I visited the church and the butcher's shop. Here behind the stable door I saw Mr. Michael Clarke who has worked here since 1964. Michael was born in the village. At sixteen he left school on a Thursday and started work the following Monday.*

Michael said his father had told him, "You can work for me if yer like, but yer do as I tell yer!" Michael worked a seven day week, killing up to 60 sheep on Sundays and Mondays. (The slaughter house out the back became redundant ten years ago.) In that time he had two holidays – one when he was 23 and the other when 58. When his dad was 80 years old he said:

"It's all yours now, do what you like." Three years later his father died. When we talked Michael spoke about the thought of closing one day. As the only surviving shop on the green I thought that this would be a pity. His meat is locally sourced and he richly deserves some encouragement. I bought some sausages to take home for my dinner. So if you visit Hartest and his little shop (with the stable door) is still open, perhaps you can do likewise!

WALK 24: LAWSHALL

Deep in the heart of the Suffolk countryside, halfway between Bury St Edmunds and Sudbury you will find Lawshall. Here is an ancient farming settlement, recorded in the Domesday Book when it had sixteen villagers, five slaves, one hundred sheep and ten cattle!

This is a circular walk that starts and ends in the village. It explores narrow lanes, treks across country estate where you will find an avenue of stately lime trees. There are no stiles.

Distance	4.5 miles or 7.2km
Time	Allow 2½ hours
Start	In the main street by The Swan
Terrain	Fairly even throughout
Map	OS Explorer 211
Refreshments	The Swan is open for food from noon until 1.30pm – except Tuesdays. Evening meals served 6-8pm
Toilets	No public toilets
Getting there	By 375 bus from Bury St Edmunds. By car from the A134 Sudbury to Bury St Edmunds road

1. Park the car near the centre of the village by the only surviving public house, The Swan. Once there were five pubs here. With your back to The Swan turn right to begin your walk past the houses of this village.

The Swan public house

2. Look out for a bright red telephone box in a lay-by on your left. It bears the sign BOOK SWAP. What a great idea for the community of readers here!

3. Continue along the road until you come to a left hand turning. This is Donkey Lane. It leads you out of the village into rolling farmland with the trees of the ancient Frithy Wood appearing to your left. The name is Saxon and the wood is recorded on a map of 1545 – for centuries it had been a haven for wildlife.

It was late spring when I walked this way; the time of year when the grass verge froths with a cloud of white cow-parsley above a tangled profusion of wild flowers; circlets of ribwort plantain; delicate

Book swap

blue forget-me-nots and the inevitable brash daubs of yellow dandelions. An orange-tip butterfly fluttered amongst them – adding to the loveliness.

4. When you see the thatch of Carpenter's Cottage (once a pub called the Carpenter's Arms) you have arrived in Hart's Green – one of Lawshall's hamlets. Here in 1899 PC Cole found a drunken Henry Moss lying by the roadside using 'foul language'. The defendant, who had previous convictions was fined two shillings and sixpence, as well as court costs.

The road was blissfully quiet and empty – not a drunkard in sight! Just far reaching views of wheat fields, lined with hedges, rising the distance smudges of hazy, blue-grey woodland.

5. A leafy track led to the listed and moated (but out of sight) Barfords, then the road pases the porch of Roseleigh, where two cheery little penguins wave from the front step.

6. Follow the lane until you come to a cherry tree – which in late spring was heavy with pink blossom, growing behind a neatly clipped hedge. This is Makin's Farm. Further along the road you will see a footpath sign pointing left and a forbidding notice which says ' Rookwood Hall – Private.'

Undaunted I checked my map and sure enough the footpath follows the drive towards Rookwood Hall. Yet more cherry trees lined the route, their discarded petals like sprinkled confetti littering the grass beneath them.

At a T- junction follow an arrow pointing left to Coldham Hall Cottage and you will quickly be rewarded with spectacular scenes of Suffolk countryside.

Above the fields a buzzard casually flapped his powerful wings once or twice, turned and slowly rose, spiralling on the thermals.

You will find yourself walking in a tunnel of trees where on a sunny day, sunlight paints dancing dappled shadows ahead of you.

7. You are now approaching Coldham Hall and will come to secure padlocked gates. There is not a footpath sign to be seen.

A friendly workman came to my rescue, and showed me a pedestrian gate which was unlocked.

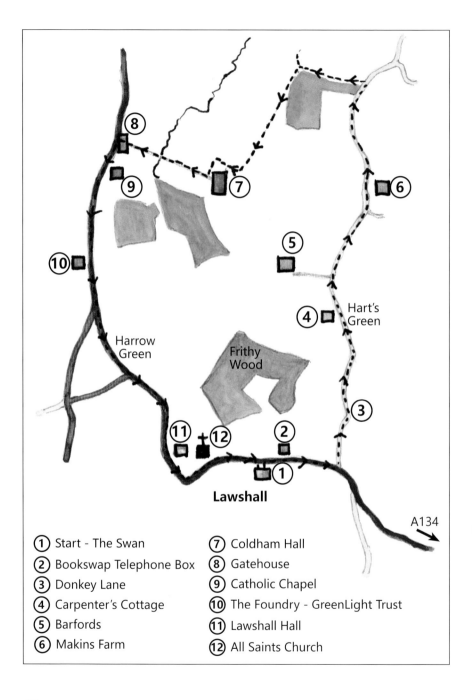

Harrow Green

Frithy Wood

Hart's Green

Lawshall

A134

① Start - The Swan
② Bookswap Telephone Box
③ Donkey Lane
④ Carpenter's Cottage
⑤ Barfords
⑥ Makins Farm
⑦ Coldham Hall
⑧ Gatehouse
⑨ Catholic Chapel
⑩ The Foundry - GreenLight Trust
⑪ Lawshall Hall
⑫ All Saints Church

Go through this gate with a lovely old farmhouse on your right and on your left you will see the tall chimneys with their ornate Tudor brickwork behind a yew hedge. This is Coldham Hall itself. The footpath takes you left to the front gates of this wonderful mansion where a sign warns you to 'Beware the Dog'! But you can pause to get a good view of the impressive building.

This was once the home of Ambrose Rookwood – a fellow conspirator of Guy Fawkes. The plan was to blow up King James I with his government. Rookwood had a stud of fine horses – the 'get-away car 'equivalent of the day. But the plot failed when Ambrose was caught and imprisoned in the Tower Of London. He was executed in 1606.

Another political figure, David Hart who was an advisor to Margaret Thatcher also lived here.

Today it has a rich and famous owner, Claudia Schiffer, the German super-model. Local people say they never see her – but hear her helicopter when it buzzes overhead.

8. Now you have a treat; a walk along the avenue of mature lime trees. All around you is parkland with established copper beech, horse chestnut and oak trees and behind you is the mansion. You too can pretend to be rich and famous!

The drive dips down to a stone bridge where lily pads float on a pond, its waters still, bar the occasional breath of wind blowing ripples across its surface. The road rises to take you to the buttressed gatehouse with its boarded-up windows. Push open a small iron gate that squeaks and creaks as if complaining at being disturbed. Climb through the gap and you will find yourself back on the road again. Turn to take a final look at the avenue before you set off left towards the village. Keep well in as there is no pavement here and a little more traffic travels this way.

The brick gatehouse

9. Soon houses appear and a tiny Catholic chapel to your left – with a heavy pan-tiled roof. It is dated 1876 and is, indeed, the oldest Catholic Mission Chapel in Suffolk. It served the Coldham Hall estate. It is dedicated to Our Lady Immaculate and St Joseph.

As I passed the chapel a friendly voice called out a greeting and I turned to see a smiling lady approaching me. I found myself in conversation with Gill, who had just been to visit her 95 year-old mother, Mary Keggin. Gill told me that her grandfather bought some land here.

"He gave one plot to my mother so she could build a house for herself. In 1955 she took out a mortgage of £3,000 with the bank and had the house built. It was an awful lot of money in those days. My mum still lives in that house – but sadly she's the only survivor of her eight siblings."

10. Keep walking by cottages until you come to the larch-clad foundry, on your right – today the home of The Green Light Trust. This is an educational charity that 'brings people and nature together'. In former days this building served as a shed for a traction engine.

Here I met Beverley Fox who readily talked about their work.

"Children who struggle within the confines of the classroom, some with mental health problems, others with profound disabilities come here to develop resilience and resourcefulness as they learn to work with nature. They coppice in Frithy Wood; build campfires, make dens or mud sculptures and other things", she told me with a note of pride in her voice.

A little further on is Lawshall Row, here you bear left to Harrow Green. This is a collection of houses, a village hall, cottages – and shaggy brown donkeys grazing in a paddock. Keep your eyes open for the village sign which carries the coat of arms of the Drury Family, who were lords of the manor in the 1500s.

11. Across the field you will soon see your next stop – All Saint's Church. Before if stands Lawshall Hall. In 1578 Queen Elizabeth I called her for dinner when she was making the Royal Progress Tour of her realm.

12. When you reach the 15th century flint church it is worth a visit. A church has stood on this spot for much longer – but this one was rebuilt with

money from the wool and cloth trade which brought considerable wealth to East Anglia at that time. In the church yard you will see lichened headstones that lean at assorted angles.

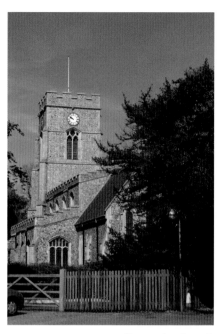

On the day I walked the clock was stuck on ten past seven. It was installed as a memorial to the twenty four soldiers from this village who never returned from the First World War – quite a loss for such a small population.

Inside All Saints was a quiet coolness. There was a corner for Godly Play where children were welcomed and visitors were invited to light a candle and say a prayer for their loved ones. I took a moment to pause and reflect.

All Saint's Church

Outside bear left to pass a modernised Victorian School – still in use today. Opposite you will see the Old Post Office (now a private home) with its dormer windows, timbered porch and pretty garden; in Spring red tulips provide a splash of colour to the scene.

Look out for interesting rooftops and chimneys on a row of cottages to your left, then Street Farm before you find yourself back where you started – at The Swan with its thatched roof and sturdy chimney stack. If you've timed it right you can buy a home-cooked meal here – or simply pop in for a sandwich.

I decided to call in for a drink and make use of the facilities. After a fair old walk, I perched thankfully on a tall bar stood and sipped fizzy lemonade and lime. The place has low black beams and I noticed that one had coins fixed upon it. I discovered that each young soldier who left to fight in the First World War left his coin – to be collected upon his return. Tragically, twenty-four coins were never reclaimed. A sobering end to my lovely walk.

WALK 25: BURES

Bures (or Bewers as it was charmingly called until 1659), where the river Stour with its lazily flowing waters, creates two villages in one; Bures St Mary on the Suffolk side and, the other, Bures Hamlet in Essex. This my longest, circular walk takes you steadily up steep tracks to wonderful views, along narrow lanes, then by a tree lined stream, and finally through the streets of Bures to end with a picnic on a grassy meadow by the river Stour.

Village sign

Distance	5.2 miles or 8.4km
Time	Allow 3 hours
Start	Free car park in Nayland road
Terrain	Very up and down – and at times leg-achingly steep
Map	OS Explorer 196
Refreshments	The village Deli for a picnic by the river. The Three Horseshoes (drink only)
Toilets	No public toilets
Getting there	The 754 bus runs from Colchester to Sudbury. Bures is on the Sudbury branch line of the London, Liverpool Street to Norwich train. Change at Marks Tey. The B1508 road from Colchester passes through Bures on its way to Sudbury

1. Near the centre of the village, not far from the church on the Nayland road is a car park and a children's playground.This is a good place to start the walk. From here turn right and stroll along Nayland road.

2. Go past the school and Head Teacher's house which stands opposite the Old Police House. In summer Wisteria House lives up to its name. You will see a crossroads where the footpath bears left, up Claypits Avenue. Leave the houses behind as it becomes a rough cart track steadily climbing the hillside.

3. It leads to a community orchard. Here are some interesting varieties of old apple trees with delightful names such as Lord Stradbroke and Coe's Golden Drop. Ignore a left hand footpath which takes you back to the village and keep pressing upwards.

When I did this lovely walk in early autumn the verges on either side were rich with flowers and nettles, as well as tall cow mumble seed heads that swayed in the gentle wind. My boots made a satisfying crunch on the stony path as I climbed. Every now and then I stopped and turned to enjoy the panoramic view of the valley below. No wonder John Constable and Thomas Gainsborough were inspired to paint in this beautiful corner of Suffolk. There are nearer rooftops, then sweeping curves of green, brown and golden fields stretching away to the far horizon and wide sky. In the valley

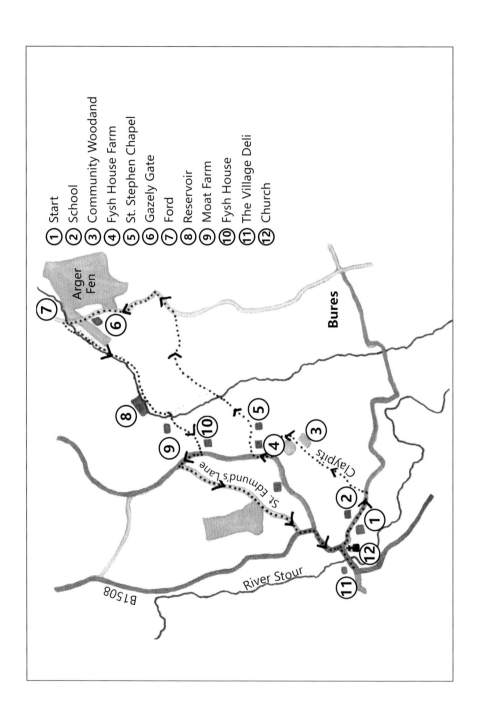

1. Start
2. School
3. Community Woodand
4. Fysh House Farm
5. St. Stephen Chapel
6. Gazely Gate
7. Ford
8. Reservoir
9. Moat Farm
10. Fysh House
11. The Village Deli
12. Church

Arger Fen

Bures

Claypits

St. Edmund's Lane

River Stour

B1508

is a tiny water mill. A distant church spire marks the hamlet of Mount Bures. The sunlight flashed on tiny, matchbox-sized cars moving noiselessly along a faraway road. To my right a bank of seeding thistles, was vibrant with bees and butterflies including tortoiseshells, and the common blue that busily flitted from flower to flower.

4. You reach the end of the track and turn left. But pause to look back. The view is stunning. Look out for Cuckoo House. At the road, turn right and after a few steps right again towards some farm buildings. Soon a lovely view appears ahead of you as the field on your left simply falls away to the stream and beyond that – more fields go on and on.

   The path curves to the right and is descending now.

   Here a green woodpecker startled, swooped his way across the valley and a jay screeched his harsh call from a tall ash tree.

5. Follow the grassy route edging the field, but first make a detour right, to take a closer look at the St Stephen's ancient chapel (1218). It has a thatched roof. There is herringbone brick work, deep buttresses and on the far side, an arched doorway. It will probably be locked.

A close up of the Water Mill

From a bench under some mature sycamore trees I simply sat and stared. A cloud of white gulls drifted across the field, like blown dandelion seeds. When I did this walk I could make out a huge dragon cut into a green pasture across the valley. There is a legend (1405) of a fierce dragon that killed sheep around Bures. Bows and arrow were unable to penetrate the beast, but after sustained attacks the creature eventually fled to a marsh land (Wormingford) and was never seen again. The dragon outline was ninety metres long and seventy metres high. It was dug to celebrate the diamond jubilee of our Queen Elizabeth in 2012. I walked back towards the chapel and spied a cherry tree. Its leaves will soon turn to vivid reds and yellows.

The footpath sign points down to the stream in the valley. There is a sturdy hawthorn hedge on your right, with shiny red berries in autumn. The path falls to a wooden stile and footbridge into the water meadows where cows stand with flicking tails. The sign reads 'Bull in field.' Take care – march (rather quickly), across the pasture taking care to dodge the cowpats.

Over another stile there is a choice; left is a short cut if you are weary, if you keep going the path climbs up a steep gradient straight across a *very* big field. Stop to catch your breath and rest a moment as you look back at the views which again are unfolding. You will eventually get to the end of the field. *(It took me about one hour to get here.)* An arrow points right and leads into a green lane. Here is a sense of quietness. Walk softly and silently. There are oak and field-maple trees, a crab apple tree (for crab apple jelly) and another wild cherry. A speckled wood butterfly alights on some blackberries. The only sound is the wind stirring in the branches and the caw of faraway rooks.

Soon you come to a road and turn left. *The autumn hedgerows are full of berries. I picked some huge ripe blackberries and tasted their sweet sourness. There is a tumbledown barn of grey weather boarding with a collapsing tiled and slate roof and gaping holes where tiles have slipped. Missing boards give shadowy glimpses of abandoned farm machinery within – a place of mystery. The doors with rusty hinges, hang at disjointed angles, and everywhere there are tall nettles and thistles growing as if to cover its shame.*

Highfields Farm is on your right. A hum of machines came from massive barns at 'W Church High Fen Seed Store'. A line of horse chestnut trees offer conkers to passing children. Further down the road you will see Arger

Fen on the right; the remnant of the ancient woodland that covered the whole of Suffolk one thousand years ago. It too deserves to be explored for there are pits (now ponds) where clay was dug and used to line timber framed houses or make bricks. Suffolk Wildlife Trust manage these woodlands and nuthatches, tree-creepers and goldcrests live there.

All I see are pigeons clattering their way noisily from trees, but if you go there late on a warm July evening you may spot glow-worms!

The road is now bordered by hedges of blackthorn with purple sloe berries (eat one if you dare)! Traveller's joy or old man's beard, drapes itself like bunting to tell us that autumn has truly arrived.

6. On the left is a house called Gazeley Gate. Part of it dates back to the late
& 16th century. It was the Ford-Keeper's House until Cromwellian times and
7. lo and behold, the ford (7) is still here. Its waters trickle across the road. Beyond it turn left along the footpath and walk by Assington Brook. On the right (up Tiger Hill) a cottage peeps out over the trees. The grassy track becomes damp and muddy after rain.

(My boots are not quite as water tight as I would like)!

The path crosses the brook several times as you follow its winding course. Here, alder trees and hazel trees (with nuts to glean) line the banks. A kiss gate makes a groaning creak, hungry for a drop of oil. Ignore a thin plank that crosses the stream near an oak tree and continue the path between a sweeping ploughed field and the brook now on your right.

8. An arrow points over another wooden plank bridge and you will see a small reservoir. Rosebay willow herb grows tall among flag rushes.

I paused to watch the orange/red dragonflies dancing over the surface of the water. They drop to touch their tail into the water then bounce along to repeat the movement, leaving a trail of ripple rings. There are also stalk-winged damsel flies and demoiselles, who usually live by slow flowing rivers. The have metallic blue broader wings.

9. You will come to a restricted by-way to Moat Farm. This is a Grade II Listed Building of 16th century origin. It is screened from walkers but can be glimpsed at the entrance gate.

I had now been walking for two hours. (I may need to mention at this point that there are NO public loos in Bures and soon I will be back among houses. Respond as you will!) As I went up the gravelly path there was the warm sweet smell of cows.

Purple knapweed now edges the road and again the view of gently rolling Suffolk fields appears between the hedges and banks of bracken. A walnut tree with smooth grey trunk may offer nuts to find if the squirrels haven't beaten you to it! Bright red berries of cuckoo pint signal danger – do not touch!

10. On the left appears a high brick wall with a crinkle (or is it a crankle)?

If you turn left down Cuckoo Hill you will soon be back in the village, but beware there is no pavement here. If you take that route it will bring you to a delightful cottage, Cuckoo's Nest, once two farm cottages. Bert Smith once lived here. He was the Village Night Soil Man who collected waste and effluent from houses, in his horse and cart and delivered it to a highly scented pit!

Instead bear right, passing a brick house called Salamander. Soon across the road is a footpath sign. Here you turn left into St Edmunds Lane, which is also called Dead Man's Lane because it is believed that a gibbet once stood there. A sweet chestnut tree with its big jagged leaves may also yield some autumn treasure, but mind the prickly cases!

There are several cottages on the right.

I catch the scent of lavender as I pass Thrush Cottage where wisteria adorns the doorway. At Planters you can buy some homemade cherry-plum jam or orange and lemon marmalade.

The lane falls steeply to the village. The sound of fast-moving traffic indicates that you are approaching a busy road. I turn left along the pavement. Look out for house names that give clues to the past; Maltings and the Old Manse of the Baptist Chapel. There is a fine 16/17th century timber framed house has a bresummer bearing carved oak leaves, men, beasts and a coat of arms. There are several houses with big windows that clearly were once shops, including The Old Bakery.

11. The Three Horseshoes (one of the few survivors of the eight pubs), serves drinks but no meals, so I turned right and crossed the river into Bridge Street where I saw a Village Deli! Food!

The Village Deli

Here there is an extensive choice of baguettes. Shall I have brie and bacon, prawn mayo and lettuce, or sun dried tom and goat's cheese? I go for the latter. While it was being prepared, I noticed bread pudding and 'love smoothies' as well as tea or hot chocolate. Later, seated on a bench overlooking the river I enjoyed my tasty lunch as I watched brown fish darting beneath the water lilies.

Later I returned to the Deli and found Sheena Hook who has lived in Bures for 59 years. She chatted about the changes; the new houses being built; the clothes factory that burned down in the 60s, and how only three shops remain – the paper shop, the Deli and the Post Office. But she brightens as she tells me how well the Village Deli is doing, especially with its home-made pastries.

"I work in two shops", she grins. "I start at the paper shop at 5am. Then come here, but we shut at 3.30pm. I wouldn't want to live anywhere else. I love it. My mum and dad lived here all their lives and my daughter lives here. I'd recommend Bures to anyone."

12. Your final stop is the stone and flint church of St Mary's. The porch of 14th century heavy timbers leads you inside, where you will see a curious stone monument with a line of small kneeling figures.

'Here liethe bvriede Sir William Waldgrave knight and his wife Elizabeth who lived together in godlye marriage 21 yeare ...'

I discover that Elizabeth had six 'sonnes' and four daughters and died in 1581, some thirty years before her husband. Ten children would not extend her life expectancy!

Village green and church

The Waldgrave family have had links with royalty and have served in government down the centuries right to this day. Sir William was knighted at the coronation of Anne Boleyn in 1545. Before him Sir Richard Waldgrave was Speaker in the House of Commons when Richard II was king in 1335. Sir Edward Waldgrave died a prisoner on the Tower of London in 1561. In 1715 James Waldgrave was a close friend of George II and in our lifetime Baron Waldgrave of North Hill serves in the house of Lords having been made Secretary of State for Health in 1990 a few days before Mrs Thatcher resigned. It is this family who have financed much of the church's construction.

Before you leave the coolness of the church, look for a carved effigy of sweet chestnut wood. It is an unknown knight who is buried somewhere in the church yard; and with me, wonder how he came to be there?

You are close to your starting place. Bear right and soon you will find yourself back in the car park.

Also from Sigma Leisure:

New Forest Walks
a seasonal wildlife guide
Andrew Walmesley

Produced to appeal to both a general audience and those with a special interest in wildlife, the book features twelve walk routes that are all fully described and accompanied by detailed sketch maps. Distances vary from 4-13 kilometres, but all the walks have shorter options available whilst some can be extended by incorporating elements of overlapping or nearby routes contained in the companion volume *New Forest Walks - a time traveller's guide.*
£12.99

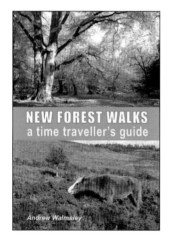

New Forest Walks
a time traveller's guide
Andrew Walmesley

Explore the New Forest with this series of 16 walks through ancient landscapes where long-forgotten bumps, hollows and moss-clad earthen banks have stories to tell of Bronze and Iron Age peoples, Romans, Normans and others who lived, worked and hunted here. Illustrated throughout with photographs that bring to life the secret past of this remarkable corner of England.
£12.99

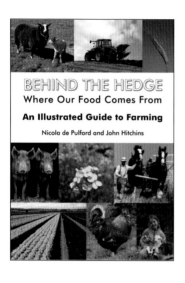

BEHIND THE HEDGE
Where Our Food Comes From
An Illustrated Guide to Farming
Nicola de Pulford & John Hitchins

Behind the Hedge is for everyone who wants to know more about the food we eat, the land it is grown and reared on, and those who farm it. It is an easy-to-follow guide which will help you identify in their natural environment our crops, fruit and farm animals, agricultural buildings and machinery, the farming landscape and the wildlife it supports. By dipping in and out of this beautifully illustrated book, you will learn to recognise the crops, farm animals and wildlife on the other side of the hedge.

£12.99

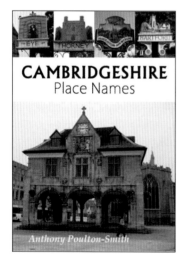

Cambridgeshire Place Names
Anthony Paulton-Smith

Ever wondered why our towns and villages are named as they are? Who named them and why? Towns, villages, districts, hills, streams, woods, farms, fields, streets and even pubs are examined and explained. The definitions are supported by anecdotal evidence, bring to life the individuals and events which have influenced the places and the way these names have developed.This is not simply a dictionary but a history and will prove invaluable not only for those who live and work in the county but also visitors and tourists, historians and former inhabitants, indeed anyone with an interest in Cambridgeshire.

£8.99

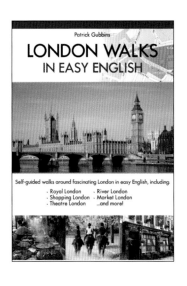

London Walks in Easy English
Patrick Gubbins

Forget the boring "walk books" that take you down quiet streets where nothing happens. *London Walks in Easy English* knows where the busy, exciting places in the capital are, and makes sure you see London life with all its colour, tradition, food, views, art, beautiful buildings and, most importantly, its sense of fun. What other book of walks takes you inside the classrooms of London University, into courtrooms to see real trials in progress, into shops to try exotic food, and to the big attractions but also to many other fascinating places that even Londoners don't know?
£9.99

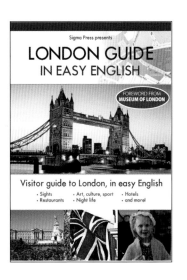

London Guide in Easy English
Patrick Gubbins

The guide covers all the capital's major and minor attractions, hotels, restaurants, parks and green areas and sporting venues, and contains a full directory of necessary information for visitors to London, including advice on working in the city. One of the book's themes is the amazing variety of activities on offer in London, some covered by no other guide, such as whitewater rafting, craft workshops, ski-ing on real snow, visits to courtrooms to watch real trials, and even how to see members of the Royal Family! Packed with exciting ideas and stunning photography, *London Guide in Easy English* is the ideal travel companion for the many visitors to London looking for a guide book written at an easy level of English.
£9.99

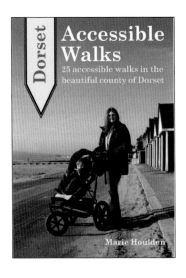

Dorset Accessible Walks
25 accessible walks in the beautiful county of Dorset
Marie Houlden

All of the walks are stile and obstacle free, with consideration given to those in wheelchairs. With walks that start from only a mile and that cover a mixture of terrain and environments, there really is something for everyone. There are even a couple of more strenuous walks for those with an all-terrain pushchair and a passion for a physical challenge!

£8.99

All-Terrain Pushchair Walks Surrey
Eleanor Simmons

A collection of 30 varied and multi-terrain pushchair friendly walks in the beautiful Surrey countryside. Enjoy gentle woodland and riverside strolls and more strenuous hikes in the Surrey hills. Each of the routes has a map, directions and essential information for fun and easy walking with babies and young children.

£8.99

All of our books are all available on-line at **www.sigmapress.co.uk** or through booksellers.

Sigma Leisure, Stobart House, Pontyclerc, Penybanc Road, Ammanford, Carmarthenshire SA18 3HP
Tel: 01269 593100 Fax: 01269 596116
info@sigmapress.co.uk www.sigmapress.co.uk